ECONOMICS AND LIBERALISM
Collected Papers

By *Overton H. Taylor*

"In this collection, substantially all the previously published writings of Mr. O. H. Taylor of Harvard are presented chronologically. Their original publication dates extend over the period 1927 to 1952. These writings not only reflect 'certain stages in the development' of Mr. Taylor's 'outlook, knowledge, and opinions,' as he suggests in the Introduction; they also establish his firm claim to a place among the creative American economists. . . . The heroic scope of this effort indicates the breadth of Mr. Taylor's interests."—*The Journal of Economic History*

"The final essay . . . reveals the thought of this singularly honest, erudite, and lively-minded writer as partaking in the unmistakable contemporary trend, both promising and dangerous, from economics toward sociology."—*Economist*

"Those who are interested in the past, as well as the future, problems of liberalism will find this collection of essays both stimulating and rewarding."—*Southern Economic Review*

$5.00

Harvard Economic Studies, 96

Harvard University Press
Cambridge 38, Massachusetts

THE CLASSICAL LIBERALISM, MARXISM, AND THE TWENTIETH CENTURY

Lectures delivered at the
Thomas Jefferson Center for Studies in Political Economy
University of Virginia

THE CLASSICAL LIBERALISM, MARXISM, AND THE TWENTIETH CENTURY

by Overton H. Taylor

HARVARD UNIVERSITY PRESS
Cambridge, Massachusetts · 1960

PREFACE

The content of this little book is the series of four public lectures that it was my privilege to give at the University of Virginia, at intervals during the autumn of 1958. I was there, on leave from Harvard, and by invitation, as "visiting scholar" in the Thomas Jefferson Center for Studies in Political Economy, recently organized at the University of Virginia. To the kind invitation of Professor James Buchanan, the Director of the Center, I owe the exceedingly pleasant and profitable time that I spent in that delightful place, and the opportunity that I had to compose and deliver these lectures. They were apparently well received by fairly large, mixed audiences composed of students and faculty members from various departments of the University and citizens of Charlottesville. And they are here reproduced, substantially as they were delivered.

It is a part of the plan of the Thomas Jefferson Center to have in residence during each semester, a different visiting scholar from some other university and part of the world to exchange ideas with its own faculty and graduate students, play a small part in the instruction of the latter, and deliver a series of several public lectures on some topic or

topics in the broad field of political economy, that is, on
the applications of knowledge and ideas in economics and
related studies—other social sciences, history, philosophy,
and political theory—to contemporary problems in the
formation and development of wise, national, public policies. The first visiting scholar to perform these functions
at the Center was Professor (Emeritus) F. H. Knight of
the University of Chicago, in the spring of 1958; and I was
the second. Our immediate successors, currently and in prospect, are various distinguished European scholars.

My idea in choosing the subject of this group of lectures
was that while Americans today are exposed to plenty of
discussion of the problems of military and diplomatic
strategy and tactics arising in the "cold war" between the
"free world" and the Communist world; they are *not* exposed to any plethora of public discussion of, nor as well
informed as they should be about, the basic philosophies
about human life and affairs which are in conflict, and the
basic issues which are at stake, in the cold war. And it
seemed to me that I, as a philosophical, political economist
and student of the relevant intellectual history, might be
able to make a small contribution in this area, to public
knowledge about and reflection upon those philosophies and
issues.

The over-all title of the entire group or series of four
lectures—"The Classical Liberalism, Marxism, and the
Twentieth Century"—reflects my view as a student of history that while the two clashing philosophies originally took
shape respectively in the eighteenth and nineteenth cen-

turies and still bear the marks of those periods, the climactic
struggle between them is occurring in the twentieth century,
in the context of partly new conditions and problems to
which neither philosophy in its traditional form is entirely
relevant; and that there may be a need "on our side" to
combine with "defense" of all that is of enduring value in
our traditional American and Western (the classical eighteenth and nineteenth century) Liberalism, efforts toward
a rational revision or modernization of that body of politico-
economic thought or doctrine.

Hence, while the first three lectures are concerned with
the histories and substance, and the current conflict, of the
two philosophies—Liberalism and Marxism—in their traditional forms, the fourth lecture is concerned with the internal problem, in or for the Liberal or free world, of
revising the traditional precepts of Liberalism as to public
policies, to better adjust them to present-day conditions and
problems. Of course, these brief, exceedingly general dis-
cussions of these immense subjects are inevitably rudi-
mentary and superficial, and can have at most only a slight,
suggestive value. The first lecture glances over an immense
expanse of intellectual history—the historic background of
the development of the classical Liberalism and its contin-
uation in or as the main American tradition of political and
economic thought and practice. The second lecture is an
effort to expound, summarily and globally, the essentials
of the "Marxism" of Karl Marx himself, and explain it as
a product of its three antecedents—"utopian" socialism, the
Hegelian philosophy of history, and Ricardian economic

theory. The third lecture—in my opinion if I may here confess this, the least satisfactory one of the four—is about what
the modern Communists have made out of Marxism or
transformed it into, some roots of the evil qualities in their
creed and outlook and actual institutions, attitudes, and
practices, and the central moral issues, as I see them, in our
conflict with them. And the fourth lecture, which may also
of course disappoint some readers, hardly gets beyond preliminary, broad and vague generalities in approaching the
topic of the needed "modernizing" revisions of the politico-
economic principles of the classical Liberalism.

To my acknowledgments, already made, of my debts to
the University of Virginia, its Department of Economics
and Thomas Jefferson Center, and Professor Buchanan, let
me add an equally warm acknowledgment of the efficient
and friendly services of the Harvard University Press and
the persons concerned there, in the publication of these lectures. I shall be very glad if any members of the wider public
which the issuance of the lectures in this form may reach,
find them of any, even slight, suggestive interest.

O. H. Taylor

Townsend, Massachusetts

July 22, 1959

CONTENTS

THE CLASSICAL LIBERALISM, MARXISM, AND THE TWENTIETH CENTURY

Chapter I ~ THE CLASSICAL LIBERALISM AND THE AMERICAN TRADITION

Let me say at the outset a few preliminary words about the scope, character, and themes of this series of four lectures. My aim is to relate all that I will say in them to the great challenge of our time, and the central issues in the conflict between our American and Western, free world's philosophy of the proper conduct of human life and affairs, and the opposing philosophy that is in control in Soviet Russia and the Communist World. But the conflict of the ideals, institutions, policies, and strategies of these two great parts of the world of today is an extremely complex, protean affair, which no one man can be wise enough to illuminate in all its aspects. Each one of us, in the effort to make his own modest contribution to the public wisdom that is needed on our side in the conduct of this struggle, must focus on those problems presented by it which the development of his own interests, knowledge, and reflections have in some measure equipped him to deal with. Now my own background in that sense is such that I must leave aside, as beyond my competence, the problems of military, world-political, and diplomatic strategy and tactics, in the struggle with world-Communism, which appear to get most of the attention paid to the struggle in our press and, I fear, by our official leaders and policy-makers. Of course, I do not by any means belittle this range of problems, which necessarily must be in the foreground of attention, much of the time, in the daily conduct of the struggle. But the matters which I feel at least better equipped to discuss, and will discuss in these lectures, and which seem to me to be in equal need of continuous, public consideration and in greater danger of being neglected, have a different character. We need not only to know how to conduct the struggle, as a contest for power in the world, with skill and success; but equally, to know and understand clearly what our struggle is about, or against and for; what the two philosophies in conflict are and mean; or how to understand the minds, beliefs, and aims and methods of our enemies, and how to spell out and apply to the current and prospective problems of our nation and the nations allied with us, our own basic convictions, or ideals for and theories of liberal democracy and the economic system of free, private, enterprises and competitive markets.

Now the two philosophies, of Communism and of liberal capitalism and democracy, are not simply of the present, nor static, fixed, immutable affairs, but developing products of past and continuing mental activity on the parts of their creators and adherents, the intellectual leaders and the masses of followers of the two great movements that are striving to reshape the world in contrary ways or lead mankind toward different destinations. Hence, I think, one excellent approach to the task of understanding the two philosophies and the central issues in the conflict between them, is the historical approach, through study of, and reflection on, the relevant developments in past and current or continuing intellectual history. The liberal theory of the free way or form of political and economic life has been developing through several centuries in Western thought and practice; and the effort to understand it, absorb and assimilate the wisdom in it, and become equipped to con- tribute to its on-going development can be aided by thoughtful study of its past development and the contri- butions made to it in the past by such great thinkers as Locke, Adam Smith, our own country's founding fathers, John Stuart Mill and others. The Communist theory of the goal of mankind's progress and the road toward it has been developed out of the dreams or visions of the first modern socialists, by Karl Marx and his disciples; and the effort to understand it, as we must if we are to oppose it intelligently and effectively, can be aided by study of the writings of Marx and of his forerunners and successors. And of course in the study of these two contrasting, past and on-going currents of thought about human affairs, we need to con- sider not only the pure, abstract philosophies themselves and their developments through time, but also the concur- rent changes of the real, social, and world conditions and problems to which the philosophies as worked out or modi- fied in each generation have been meant to refer and be relevant. It is possible that neither most of the liberal nor most of the Marxist thinkers of today have, for their respective purposes, sufficiently adjusted their inherited, traditional, intellectual visions to the newer, recently and currently emerging, real conditions and problems of our time; and there may be a need on our side to work out a more fully modernized form of the liberal philosophy than is yet known or at all widely prevalent. My purpose then, in this series of lectures, is to offer a general, broad survey of the kind suggested by the title of the series: The Classical Liberalism, Marxism, and The Twentieth Century.

The first lecture will be about the Classical Liberalism and the American Tradition. The central or main, American tradition of political and economic thought—the typical "American dream" or vision of the good, democratic society and state and economic system of free, private enterprises and competitive markets—has been or become the world's main, continuing development of the social philosophy—originally formed in or by the eighteenth century Enlightenment, out of many elements of the still much older cultural inheritance of Western Europe—which I think it is proper to call "the classical liberalism." And I shall begin with a brief outline of what seem to me the essentials, and some of the main and most illuminating phases of the history or past development, of this philosophy as the traditional basis of the American outlook. Then my second lecture will be about the main ideas of Karl Marx, and their historic sources, in earlier socialist thought, in the German philosopher Hagel's philosophy of history which Marx took over and transformed, and in the system of economic theory of the English classical economist, Ricardo, which Marx united

or fused with his vision of all history and its future con-
tinuation, and his socialist vision of its goal, and transformed
and developed into his own economic theory of the structure, working, evolution, inner conflicts and dilemmas, and
impending doom of the economic system and social order
and civilization which he named "capitalism." Then after
thus outlining in the first two lectures respectively, the
classical liberal and traditional American social philosophy
and that of Marx, I shall try, in the third lecture, to bring
the two philosophies as more recently, further developed
into mutual confrontation and discuss the main issues, as I
see them, in their conflict in the world of today. And finally,
in the fourth and last lecture, I shall speak of the unfinished
task that I think lies before us, of revising and developing
our liberal philosophy into one more adequate for coping
with the crucial problems of the modern world.

You may well think that, in spite of my modest-sounding
words at the outset about limiting the scope of these lectures,
I am in fact proposing to undertake a very much too ambitious task. But of course I shall not pretend to offer about
these vast subjects anything more than a very broad but very
undetailed, or "bird's-eye," view of them. And I think that
such a view may have its own positive value, of course at
the price of its great limitations. It is a source of weakness
as well as of strength in very much modern thought, inquiry,
and discussion that it carries specialization and the pursuit
of thorough mastery of limited subjects to the point of
failing to achieve or retain any true, broad visions of the
larger, whole subjects of which they are parts, or the ade-

quate, general perspectives which are necessary if we are to form well-balanced judgments. To deal thoroughly with all the matters to be touched on in these lectures, I would need not only a large multiple of the amount of time I will have and use, but also an ideal combination of the different skills and kinds of knowledge of the world's economists, sociologists, political scientists, historians, philosophers, and moralists. In a sense I shall be venturing to speak in all those rôles at once, throughout, or invading the fields of all those specialties, in an effort to suggest the kind of all-around understanding that I think is needed, of the great issues at stake in the conflict of the liberal and Communist visions for the future of mankind. Having neither enough time nor enough competence to offer more than a few suggestive generalities, I will try only to do that, and hope that my suggestions may help some of you to go on much farther in your own independent studies and reflections.

* * *

In coupling together closely as I do, the clusters of ideas and ideals that I call the American tradition and the classical liberalism, I am of course not using the word "liberalism" in just the special sense or meaning which it has acquired in its common usage in the last generation in political life and thought in the United States. That is, I do *not* identify "liberalism" with the cult of the Rooseveltian New Deal and Harry Truman's Fair Deal, nor with enthusiasm for the trend toward the welfare state or what might be called "humanitarian big government," as opposed to the older American tradition in favor of more limited government or *laissez faire* or "rugged individualism." In fact, and in spite of the fact that the views and attitudes of our remaining devotees of that older tradition are now generally described —correctly enough in one sense—as conservative or even reactionary, the old liberal ideal was a society of largely free or ungoverned or only self-governed, independent individuals, living together under and jointly supporting a small, simple, inexpensive government having only a quite limited sphere of authority or a few quite limited powers and functions. This was the original form of what I call the classical liberalism. My subject here is the latter, and not the somewhat different, modern, new, or revised American "liberalism" of our time. I do not, however, by any means entirely reject or exclude that other, present-day, reforming liberalism, or regard it as something wholly or fundamentally alien and opposed to the older, American and classical liberalism to be considered here. To my mind the newer liberalism that is generally so called in our politics today is an as yet not fully formed, a so far partly right and partly misdirected, groping or fumbling effort to revise or modify the old or classical, liberal philosophy and program, to better adapt it for coping with the newer social conditions and problems of our time, and I will speak about all this in my fourth and final lecture.

Let me now say what I think has been and is—for it is still very much alive—the classical-Western and traditional-American liberalism. I think of it as a philosophy, or reasoned, reasonable faith about, or vision of, the kind of system of all human institutions and relations, and code of ethics for the conduct of human societies and their members, best adapted to or required to best satisfy the human nature and needs of mankind; or required to enable all human beings, as individuals, to develop toward realization of their own best potentialities, and achieve or lead good, happy, human lives of voluntary, mutual service to each other. The central ideal of the liberal philosophy is adequate and equal liberty or freedom for all persons severally; freedom for everyone to pursue in his own ways his own freely chosen ends, and freedom from coercion or control by others; for each and every person the greatest amount of such freedom which can be made consistent or compatible with the same amount of it for everyone else; and in all relations and dealings among the free individuals, mutual respect for, and conduct consistent with, each other's rights or proper freedoms, and voluntary cooperation to create, develop, and support the public institutions, laws, and policies, or the kind of political, legal, economic, and social order, likely to work best or have the best results for the freedom and the common welfare of all. Liberalism is libertarianism, or concern on the part of all for the liberty of all and the harmony among all without which the conflicts among them would expose the weak to enslavement by the strong. A society is a liberal society insofar as it aims toward, and approximates or approaches realization of, the ideal of being or becoming an harmonious society of free individuals.

This ethical philosophy for and of good civil societies of free citizens has been developing throughout the history of Western civilization, from remote antiquity to the present day; although its beginnings in antiquity, the Middle Ages, and the first modern centuries were minor and partial, imperfect suggestions generally in more or less conflict with the main, prevailing tendencies of thought and practice in those times. The greatest or main development of the liberal philosophy and its rise to the position of the currently, generally prevailing climate of opinion in the Western world, occurred in the eighteenth century in the general, intellectual movement and movement for many social reforms which thought of itself as, and came later to be called, the Enlightenment. Now the founding fathers of our country and its federal constitution were typical men of the Enlightenment, who fully shared and contributed to, or helped to spell out and apply, the liberal, libertarian philosophy and did very much to form the fabric and the spirit of our national society in accordance with it. Moreover, the character and situation of this country and its people then and thereafter were such that this ideal vision of the good liberal or free society has had here an almost uniquely full and lasting influence, unobstructed by the old persisting and the later new oppositions which have complicated the modern histories of freedom in most other countries. But before saying more about the great eighteenth century development and the subsequent, continuing, American development of the classical liberalism, let my first say a few words about some of the very old or early contributions made toward it in far past times by elements of ancient Greek thought and Roman practice, by Christianity and some elements of medieval thought and practice, and by the Renaissance, the Reformation, and the seventeenth century developments in philosophy, the sciences, and political and economic life and thought which laid the foundations for the eighteenth century Enlightenment.

The first, very essential elements of the liberal philosophy that as a whole was only to arise in a much later and different time and world arose first within, or as elements of, the moral and political wisdom of the ancient Greeks and Romans who first created Western civilization. We owe jointly to the brilliant, intellectual genius of Greek thinkers and the practical genius of Roman lawyers, statesmen, and administrators, our basic working ideas of the imperative requirements of impartial, reciprocal justice among men; of the state as created by and to serve the people; and of the virtues required in a society and in its members to make it a good society and their lives, good lives, marked by an all-around harmony or balance of fulfillments of all of the important, human needs of all—the basic, working ideas on these vital topics which have ever since been at work in the evolutions of all Western civilized societies. At the same time, those peoples and communities of the ancient-classical, Mediterranean world had faults or limitations which prevented any complete development by them of the universalistic, humane idealism and ethical wisdom of the later, classical-modern liberalism at its best. The Greeks and Romans had or practiced, and even their best, humane thinkers generally approved of, slavery—enslavement of the enemy aliens conquered or captured in their wars, and slave populations doing much of the hard or menial, necessary

work which supported the free citizens or at least the upper-
class gentlemen among them in partial idleness, and gave
them the leisure to cultivate their minds, philosophy, the
sciences, the fine arts, and statecraft, or enabled them to be
mainly thinkers, talkers, writers, artists, moralists, and politicians. Moreover, the limitations of their moral insights
which enabled those gentlemen of antiquity to own and
use fellow human beings as slaves with easy consciences had
other results or expressions also. There was generally in
them much provincial, ethnic, and class pride or arrogance,
which led them to look down upon all other peoples, with
other cultures, as barbarians, and in only a lesser degree to
look down upon even those of their fellow-citizens who,
though above the level of their slaves, were in middle and
lower, laboring ranks or classes below themselves, as inferior beings. They lacked the later, Christian ideas of God
as the impartially affectionate Father of all human beings,
and the universal brotherhood of all men or all members
of the human family, and the equal and infinite worth of
all of them as individuals in the sight of God; and of the
duality of all human nature, the potential goodness and
potential sinfulness in all of us alike, and the duty of everyone to cultivate the twin virtues of humility and charity or
to avoid all self-exaltation and harsh judgments against
others. Basically, I think, the ancient-classical outlook relied
too exclusively upon intellectual cultivation alone to insure
the best conduct of human life and affairs, and did not
sufficiently recognize the importance of good-heartedness, or
development in all men of the right feelings, emotions, or

affections as the true, fundamental mainsprings of our conduct. Thus, although Graeco-Roman thought about the relations among men and their proper treatment of each other admirably developed the ideal of justice, it did not get beyond that really negative ideal (not injuring anyone) or anticipate the later and higher Christian ideal of positive love or good will in the heart of everyone toward everyone.

Hence, although the best ethical, social, and political wisdom of pre-Christian, classical antiquity made essential contributions to the eventual development of the universal, liberal humanism or humane liberalism which is my theme; it remained for Christianity or Christian ethics to make a second, equally important set of contributions that supplemented and corrected the deficiencies of those derived from Greek and Roman antiquity. The classical vision was a rational vision of the good order or balance to be sought in human lives and societies, analogous to the self-maintaining balance of forces in the natural universe; an all-around balance of satisfactions of all the natural desires of all individuals, and balance of growths and harmonious functionings of all sides of their natures, to the over-all benefit of all of them severally and of the community. And to this, Christian thought-and-feeling added its own super-rational, or more and better than merely rational, religious-intuitive vision of the divine love literally for all men equally and not for any select groups alone or especially; and the need to extend the impartial balance of freedoms, opportunities, helps, and encouragements, literally to all men alike, everywhere; and to make this possible, the need of everyone for self-reform, with divine help, of the morally imperfect, basic impulses of his nature itself. Now it was the great work of the medieval European, Roman Catholic Christian scholars and philosophers, Schoolmen, or scholastic doctors, to construct their comprehensive, admirable synthesis of these two visions—that already achieved and expressed in antiquity, in Greek philosophy and in Roman law, and that which was the peculiar, additional contribution of the Christian faith. I want now to glance at this medieval scholastic, at once classical and Christian outlook, and the limitations imposed on it by the social realities around it in its time and world, which still kept it from quite achieving the moral level of the liberal vision of a still later time.

The principal architect of the great medieval, scholastic synthesis of the ancient-classical and the Christian moral-social philosophies or visions was Saint Thomas Aquinas, and this great system of thought accordingly is called Thomism. Now in Thomism, as in the ancient-classical, Aristotelian and Stoic philosophies, and as again in the later, liberal philosophy of the eighteenth century Enlightenment, a central and all-pervading idea was that of a cosmic-and-ethical system of natural law or natural laws, to which all the processes of nature or the universe apart from human life and affairs do conform, and to which all human conduct and the formations, forms, and functionings of all human, civil societies ought to conform, and do at least tend to conform insofar as men develop and use or are guided by the best rational and moral wisdom which their human nature in its healthy state has the power and inclination to achieve and use. Saint Thomas says, in essence, that *all things and creatures are governed by natural laws, ordained by Providence for their preservation and that of the good order of the universe of which they are parts. And man, who as a rational being is himself, by nature, provident, participates in this reign of natural law in a peculiarly excellent way. To him alone it is given to know, by the use of his reason, what are the natural laws for his conduct, obedience to which is best for the welfare of each man and of mankind, and to be free and able to obey them, voluntarily.* It is true, however, that for Saint Thomas, this rationalistic and naturalistic part of his philosophy, which came down to him out of pre-Christian Greek philosophy, was in a measure qualified and complicated by some of the tenets of his Christian faith. Human nature had been partially corrupted by "the fall of man" or Adam's sin or disobedience and the presence in all his descendants of the strain of moral weakness designated as "original sin," and the effects of this included both a degree of dimming of the "natural light" of human reason, and the presence in all men of perverse or evil desires or passions capable of prompting or producing conduct plainly contrary to even their limited, rational, moral insights. Hence for imperfect human beings as they are, the natural part of the body of divine law for their moral government, that is, the part which it is in their power to discover and obey without supernatural help, is not fully adequate but needs to be supplemented by the higher, supernaturally revealed, Christian laws or commandments, accessible or evident not to reason but to faith, or above reason though not contrary to reason, and to be obeyed only with the help of supernatural, divine grace. Yet St. Thomas attached very much importance to the purely natural and rational system or part of the complete system of moral or divine law, and in the main appealed only to this part in discussing the secular or worldly affairs and problems of human, civil societies, or developing his social political, and economic thought. The natural moral law or code was to be or should be embodied or spelled out in human law as formulated by rulers in consultation with the natural leaders of, and spokesmen for, their subjects, and interpreted by judges in the courts, and enforced at need by officials. But "human law" was held to be valid or binding only insofar as it was morally reasonable or natural law, not made or decreed by the arbitrary wills of men in power, but found or discovered, agreed on, and accepted by the reason common to all reasonable men, or in other words by the moral common sense of each community. The highest rulers, no less than their humblest subjects, were held to be under, not above, the law, which defined the reciprocal, natural rights and duties among all, or the requirements of justice from all and to all and of the best welfare of all, both severally and collectively.

In its abstract principles this ethico-legal, central part of Thomism—which still is fully alive today as a vital part of the special culture of the world's Roman Catholic community—was not and is not really radically unlike the ethico-legal, central part of the philosophy of later growth which I am calling the classical liberalism. But in the more detailed or concrete, medieval applications to specific problems, the Thomist version of the idea of the system of ethical natural law got construed generally in no very liberal, but rather in a fairly conservative and often semi-authoritarian, spirit as on the whole sanctioning the existing, actual, feudal, and hierarchical social order in medieval Europe, which to modern liberal minds appears in retrospect to have been a neither Christian nor rational system, but one that grossly over-enlarged the freedom, privileges, and powers of the few in upper-class positions and imposed severe, unjust restrictions on the freedoms, rights, and opportunities of the middle-class men of business and the humble peasants, serfs, and artisans, in equal violation of both the Christian ideal of equal love or concern for all human beings, and the ancient-classical, rational ideal of impartial justice. But it is, alas, a universal fact that whenever a good set of ideals has become prevalent and is at work within an actual, not-so-good society, as an influence tending to improve the latter, there is always also a strong counter-tendency of the familiar, established features of the morally imperfect, actual society, and the narrow interests and resulting, biased minds and feelings of most members of the dominant classes or groups in it, to produce a prevailing, distorted interpretation and set of applications of the ideals themselves, which does more to sanction and support than to reform the existing order. In medieval Europe the ideal principles of the philosophy expounded by its educated leaders thus got distorted in their detailed applications by the ties of the sympathies and interests of those leaders with the feudal lords, to the advantage of the latter and the disadvantage of the common people. In the western Europe and America of the nineteenth century, the ideal principles of the classical liberalism likewise tended to get distorted or misconstrued and misapplied in the ruling business and political communities, to the advantage of the persons and groups with the most influence within those communities and the disadvantage of their less influential competitors and of the masses of workers, farmers, and consumers. Liberal criticism of the outlook and the practices which prevailed in the Middle Ages should be restrained or tempered by a humble awareness of the very great difficulty of preserving the purity and the proper, effective, and genuine reforming power of any idealism, including liberalism. Moreover, a fair view of the historic facts in the medieval case must recognize, I think, that while the philosophy which prevailed, as it was generally construed and applied, did too much to sanction and support and not enough to reform the existing, highly morally imperfect, feudal order, still it did not entirely or only sanction and support that order, but at the same time did do a good deal to soften, civilize, and moralize or humanize it, or modify its worst potential features. The abstract principles of the philosophy itself lived on in European thought, and later made a very large and important contribution to those of the classical liberalism. In the much later (eighteenth century) struggle between those who wanted to perpetuate the by then much changed and deteriorated, old regime as developed from its medieval origins, and the men of the Enlightenment who wanted to reform or revolutionize that old regime and emancipate all whom it oppressed, the amount of disagreement between the medieval Thomist and the liberal philosophy of the rational and natural moral and social order was exaggerated, and the really large amount of common ground between them was denied or unrecognized or at best grossly underestimated on both sides. But in fact the liberal philosophy of the Enlightenment was not the antithesis, but a revival and limited revision and new, further development, of the basic ideas about the true, moral order to be realized in human lives and societies, carried on from medieval Thomism.

Yet before I can say more about the later, liberal revival-and-revision of those basic ideas, I must first speak briefly about a number of intervening developments, in the long interval between the thirteenth century and the eighteenth, which in different ways contributed both to the temporary decline and the need for a revival of those ideas, and to the eventual, liberal revival and revision of them. In the Renaissance there was a trend toward a more complete and more nearly pure or exclusive renewal of the ancient-classical, rationalistic and naturalistic outlook, which tended in a measure to divorce it from distinctively Christian beliefs and ideals and to almost discard or at least deemphasize the latter. In the Protestant Reformation there was, on the other hand, an effort to return to the original, primitive, "pure" form or kind of Christianity and strip away and discard or at least deemphasize all of the merely human, inferior wisdom which the (in Protestant eyes) too worldly Church

and culture of medieval Catholic Christendom had com-
mingled with it. Thus there tended to come about for a
time, in that epoch of the Renaissance and the Reformation,
as unfortunate breakdown, or separation of and opposition
between the two halves, of the medieval union of the
ancient-classical, philosophical or rational, and the Christian,
religious-and-ethical, visions of the right social order and
way of life for mankind. The results were in some ways
retrogressive in both cases. In much of the mainly secular
or nonreligious, semipagan, or less than fully Christian
thought which developed in and from the Renaissance,
there was some loss of or decline from those feelings and
ideals of the universal, equal, and infinite worths or dignities
of all individuals and the proper, equal rights of all and
mutual love or good will among all that have been the
essence of the Christian contribution to both the medieval
and the liberal outlook. And in much of the early, rather
fundamentalistic, Protestant-Christian thought of the Reformation era, there was a loss of, or decline from, the high
respect for human reason and for human nature, without
which the Christian contribution cannot play its proper,
effective role within all intellectual life and culture. Then
also, in the slightly later, intellectual revolution that laid
the modern foundations of philosophy and the natural and
social sciences, or at least began to give all those inquiries,
instead of their ancient or their medieval characters, their
modern, progressive, rational-and-empirical characters—in
one early phase of this development there was for a time
a tendency toward another breaking up or breaking down

of the unity of Western intellectual and spiritual culture as a whole, along a different line of cleavage. That is, there was then for a time, as there has been again recently, a widespread tendency to make all inquiries or sciences solely studies of existing actualities and actual processes, and the causes of effects and the means of attaining all human ends; and divorce them from ethical reflection or the search for a rational vision of the right or good ends or goals to be sought by mankind; and give up such reflection or that search as nonscientific and hence futile or chimerical. Moreover, there went along and interacted with that intellectual trend toward an amoral or morally neutral, hardheaded and hard-boiled realism, a concurrent trend in the world of action and the actual conduct of affairs that tended to express or manifest the same spirit. The rather Machiavellian princes, statesmen, and merchant-princes or business leaders of that age—the seventeenth century—as a rule were mainly concerned, not with efforts to discover and obey the normative principles of divine or natural, moral law, but only with efforts to discover and apply the principles of expediency that would show them how to attain, in the most efficient ways, their worldly ends—individual and national wealth and power. Thus the early-modern European "old regime" or social order became in its old age, in the seventeenth and eighteenth centuries, on the whole, more harsh, corrupt, depraved, and cynical than it had been in its medieval childhood. And so the men of the liberal "enlightenment," in their revolt against that existing order and the ideas and attitudes of its supporters, tended to think of themselves as creating an entirely new and uniquely valid cosmic and social and moral philosophy, in full opposition especially to all of the inheritance from the Middle Ages, which still lingered on within their epoch's culture. But in fact, I think, they created their indeed partly new and indeed on the whole improved, superior philosophy with no little aid from that very inheritance or included in their liberal philosophy —with their own revisions and along with other, ancient and modern ideas which had lain beyond the limits of the knowledge of the medieval thinkers—much of the original, true essence of the medieval social-moral vision, which had come to be largely absent from the outlook of their opponents, the defenders, in their time, of the old regime.

The real beginnings, however, of the Enlightenment and of the liberal revival-and-revision of that high social-moral vision lie farther back, within the same epoch (of the sixteenth and seventeenth centuries) which witnessed mainly the decline of which I have been speaking. Even while that decline was going on in many of the currently most influential, intellectual and ruling class circles, the first liberal thinkers and forerunners or initiators of the liberal "enlightenment" already were at work in other quarters. Grotius and his successors were developing the liberal philosophy of natural-and-international law or justice, mainly out of the same ancient-classical idea of the system of ethical "natural law" which had been central also in the medieval philosophy of St. Thomas Aquinas. And in late seventeenth century England, her great philosopher, Locke, whose thought was the most important, single, immediate source of the eighteenth century Enlightenment, wrote the essay on civil government, which was the first great classic statement of the simple, fundamental ideals or principles of liberal democracy; and the statement that became, a century later, a principal source of the guiding ideas of both *les philosophes* in France, who gave the French Revolution its philosophy, and of our American nation's "founding fathers." In my very limited time now I make these references to Grotius and Locke only, among all the forerunners or first initiators of the liberal "enlightenment" because I think of Grotius and Locke as standing respectively for the two main parts of the philosophy of liberalism: the international part, affirming and spelling out the principles of justice which should regulate all dealings and relations among nations, governments, and peoples, and insure to all the citizens of all nations alike, wherever they may go or do business in the world, the same just rights and opportunities; and the domestic, intranational part, affirming and spelling out the principles that should be embodied in the effective constitution of every national society and state to insure alike to all individual persons living within it the same generous, just, and equal freedoms, rights, and opportunities in all their dealings and relations with each other and with their country's government. I conceive the liberalism which this lecture is about as liberal individualism and internationalism; the vision of a world of free or independent, but in their mutual relations peaceful, just, and friendly nations, all severally made up of free individuals, living in freedom and justice under limited, liberal governments, all steadily rendering and administering impartial justice to, and impartially protecting all the proper freedoms of, all individuals who as citizens or as aliens are within their jurisdictions. And I think of Grotius as the great, early prophet of liberal internationalism and of Locke as the great, early prophet of liberal individualism, who once and for all announced its gospel of the equal, natural rights of all individuals and the duty of each nation's government to respect and impartially protect those rights inherent in the humaneness of all individuals within its borders.

Now I must in passing mention a striking passage in Locke's essay on civil government which shows the almost direct descent of his conception of the system of ethical natural law and the natural rights of all individuals from that of St. Thomas Aquinas. The passage that I speak of is a long, approving quotation from a book by a sixteenth century English writer, Richard Hooker, *and* what is quoted from that is Hooker's approving quotation of a passage from St. Thomas Aquinas. The substance of this passage, identical in Aquinas, Hooker, and Locke, is to me of great interest; substantially, it runs as follows. *Since all men share the same human nature, they all ought in reason to love one another, and grant to each other all of the rights which they severally feel entitled to claim for themselves.* But now also, as much as I want to emphasize this striking evidence of basic agreement of the ethical spirit of the Lockeian, liberal individualism with that of medieval Thomism, I want equally to emphasize and bring out or suggest an important difference of the liberal from the Thomist vision of the way in which the kind of ordering of social life demanded by this ethical spirit can best be realized. The difference that I now speak of shows up most clearly in the field of economic theory and the related, normative principles of proper governmental or public, economic policy.

Thomist and all medieval thought held that, for protection of the just rights of all in their business dealings with each other, there must be a great deal of direct, public, legal regulation of all such dealings or transactions to ascertain or determine and enforce in every case the just price of everything sold and bought in every market and to make sure that no man would ever be allowed to obtain any excessive or unjust profit or gain at another's expense. There was much justification for this effort to insure economic justice among men through legal regulation of all business dealings under the conditions that existed in medieval Europe—the nonexistence in that world of well-organized and wide or extensive, competitive markets, widespread, rapid, and inexpensive communication and transportation, and numerous, alternative opportunities open to all individuals. Monopolies were so common in that world that opportunities to buy or sell elsewhere on fairer terms were generally absent, and opportunities to gouge or exploit the customers or suppliers who had no alternatives and were at your mercy were plentiful, and legal regulation of all the monopolies perhaps offered the only possibility of approximating economic justice. But the approximation that could be achieved in that way was never very good or near to real justice because the authorities who had to decide on or

prescribe and enforce the so-called just prices were inevitably
exposed to strong pressures from the monopolies—the medieval guilds, or tight, monopolistic organizations of the local
merchants and craftsmen everywhere—and were rarely able
to be really impartial or objective or to ascertain that elusive
thing, the truly just price. The much better road toward
economic justice, where or if this becomes available, lies
through development of an economic system of wide, free,
or open, competitive markets, large numbers of rival enterprises in all fields of activity, and easy mobility of all producers, capital, workers, products, money, and consumers
out of ruts that are or become disadvantageous for them and
into the best-rewarding employments or markets. Such an
economic system, insofar as it can be realized, can be or
function as a self-adjusting mechanism, in which all gravi-
tate toward their best opportunities, supplies of all goods and
services develop in response and adjustment to the demands
for them, all prices are kept by competition close to the just
levels determined by the necessary costs of producing things
and by their utilities or values to consumers, and all con-
tributors to production are rewarded in accordance with the
competitive market values of their contributions. The historic evolution, however, away from the medieval system of
regulated monopolies and toward realization of the liberal,
competitive, economic order has involved not only a long,
slow, complex evolution of the structure of the real economic world itself, but also an evolution of thought about
it, or economic theory, and of institutions and public policies,
affected in each epoch by the currently prevailing mode of

thought and affecting the evolution of the real economic system. An essential role has been played by the development of economics as a science, in its own field working not to formulate the principles or precepts of ethical natural law or justice, but to discover the economic laws of the potential processes of an economic system in which the individuals, firms, and households choose the courses of action which pay them best—within the limits of free choice allowed by the society's effective ethics and legal system—and by so acting affect in definite, discoverable ways each other's subsequent opportunities and actions, and thus generate the operational processes of the economic system. If there are such processes, which go on according to their own laws, and enough is known about them, then the public, ethical, political, and legal task is to so develop the society's institutions and effective moral code and the structure of its economic system that the natural working of that system's economic laws or processes will result in economic justice among all and the greatest welfare of all severally and collectively.

The development, however, of the modern science of the economic laws of the working or functioning of a business-enterprises-and-markets economy began in that epoch of relative ethical or moral decline that I spoke of earlier, between the heyday of Thomism and that of the classical liberalism, when the chief current concern was not with any philosophy of morality and justice, but only with developing the pure and applied, predictive sciences and discovering how best to win in the struggles of nations and of business groups for wealth and power. Hence the earliest phase of the growth of modern economic theory and policy was the growth of what historians call "mercantilism"—a body of theory as to how the working of a nation's economy could be so regulated by its government as to maximize the resulting wealth and power of that national state and do so at the cost, as far as possible, of rival nations. While the medieval effort to regulate all business dealings had aimed, in theory at least, at the goal of economic justice among men, this later and different, "mercantilist" kind of governmental regulation of all business openly aimed only at increasing national wealth and power for use in the contests with foreign rivals and cared nothing about justice or the equal rights of individuals. It was only in the later, next phase of the progress of economic science, in the second half of the eighteenth century and in the hands of the Physiocrats and Adam Smith, that scientific theory of the operational processes of national economies got combined or coordinated with the Lockeian or liberal theory of the precepts of ethical natural law, the natural rights of all men, and the duties of all governments to respect and protect those rights of all. The result was the liberal, economic-and-ethical theory of political economy, as the art of so developing the legal framework around the economy that its natural processes, engendered by the spontaneous actions of all as free individuals, would tend toward universal prosperity and justice.

Our own country began its development as an independent nation exactly in the heyday and under the full influence of the classical liberalism, and the great American effort has continued to be aimed at building and operating our society along those liberal lines. There also emerged, however, out of the eighteenth century Enlightenment, and began its own development in the early nineteenth century, the rival philosophy of socialism—the vision of a world to be organized and ordered not through individual freedom for all but through collective ownership and planning. And a little later Karl Marx began the development of the special, Marxist brand of socialist thought and endeavor, which has led in our time to the strong challenge offered by the modern Communist disciples of Marx to our liberal civilization.

Chapter II ~ THE SOCIALIST TRADITION,
AND KARL MARX'S VISION OF THE
HISTORY AND DESTINY OF MANKIND

Tonight we are concerned with the general character of, and main ideas in, the intellectual system created by Karl Marx. Now, of course, I cannot convey in a single lecture anything more than a very faint and superficial glimmer of understanding of this vast, complex, and obscure system of ideas, which is Marxism. But I think an attempt to give a condensed overview of it all may be worth while in spite of the very great limitations this is bound to have. I am more concerned with the question of bias in the kind of outline or interpretation I can give, and I must say a preliminary word about this. I must freely confess that I do not love Marx and may not be able, though I shall do my best, to describe his doctrines with as much sympathetic understanding as is necessary in or for a decent objectivity. But I think few things are more important today than the effort, on the parts of all of us who are and will remain opposed to much that is in Marxism or has grown out of it, to understand it all as fully and fairly as we can. For this strange, great system of thought has shown such power as few intellectual productions in all human history have had to inspire or incite whole nations to both violent and persistent efforts to transform the world. And if we who feel impelled and bound by our own deepest convictions to oppose the aims and methods of the modern disciples of Marx are to oppose them intelligently and effectively, I think we must first acquire a deeper and truer understanding than is yet at all widespread among us of the ideas behind those aims and methods, and the grounds and plausibilities of these ideas, and the secret of their power to grip and move a great part of mankind.

At the same time, we also need to make a distinction between the Marxism of Marx himself and what Lenin and his successors, the leaders of the modern Communists, have made out of it. I think it is fair to hold Marx himself partly, but only partly, responsible for the worst, evil things in the creed and code of conduct of this main group of his modern followers. Karl Marx was a complex man or several men at once. He was a truly great scholar and thinker no matter what or how we feel about him. Also he was on the whole a civilized, humane man, whose indignant sympathy with the misery of millions of humble toilers in the world of his time, together with his theories that capitalism was the cause of their misery and that socialism would be their only way of salvation from it, inspired his zeal to hasten the destruction of the one and the arrival of the other. Finally he was a passionate, often violently emotional man, whose emotions became so fused or blended with his intellectual views or doctrines as to give the emotions an unnatural permanence and communicability to his disciples and to give the doctrines, suffused with those emotions, a tremendous explosive power. Now in the hands of later disciples—with less than their master's genuine scholarly and intellectual abilities and interests, and little or none of his civilized humaneness, and with other backgrounds and experiences of their own disposing them to attitudes and actions which he never contemplated—the impassioned system of thought-and-feeling that he passed down to them has understandably become a corrupted or degraded version of what left his hands, and the evil gospel of a system of brutality, deceit, and tyranny that he himself would surely have repudiated. At the same time, the effort to understand modern Communism must begin with the effort to understand the original vision and doctrines, the mixture or blend of the insights and the errors or fantasies, of Marx himself.

Now there were three different, antecedent sources that, as developed and changed by Marx, became components of his thought. I think it is best to take these up in succession and consider each first in its original, pre-Marxian form and then as it entered, with his alterations, into Marx's system. One of these three things was socialism or the socialist vision of the goal of all human progress—of the good, perfected, socialist society and civilization of the distant future. Then a second essential part of Marxism is its theory of the process and pattern of all human history, past and current and still to come, or the total process of all human, social evolution, and the plan for cooperation with that process—or intelligent, effective, political action within and upon it to both hasten and direct or guide it —that Marx fashioned by taking over and revising radically in one respect, the philosophy of history already previously worked out by the great German philosopher, Hegel. And the third essential part of Marxism is Marx's transformation and development of the system of economic theory of the English classical economist Ricardo, which Marx made over into his own economic theory of the structure, working, evolution, internal conflicts and dilemmas, and impending doom of the economic system and social order and civilization which Marx was the first to name "capitalism." Ricardo's theory of economics had been formed within the context of, and allied with, the social philosophy of the classical liberalism and gave on the whole a friendly or favorable, although not too rosy, view of the liberal or free and competitive form of "capitalism" or the business economy. But Marx transferred Ricardo's theory of economics out of its original, liberal context, into the radically different context of his own revised-Hegelian philosophy of the history and socialist vision of the destiny of mankind; and with the help of those new adjuncts, he changed the economic theory that he borrowed into a severely adversely critical analysis of evolving "capitalism," claiming to show that and how it was doomed to destroy itself and prepare the way for the inevitable triumph of world-wide "socialism." Let us look, then, successively, at these three antecedents and parts of Marxism: the socialist vision, the philosophy of history, and the economic theory and critique of capitalism.

Recorded expressions of bits of more or less socialistic thought and feeling can be found scattered throughout the history of Western civilization. But the socialist vision and movement seeking to realize it first began to take on fairly definite forms and a fairly serious importance in the very late eighteenth and very early nineteenth century; and the main development has gone on from that time to the present. The oldest historic sources of the vision were, I think, certain exceptional and extreme developments or versions of ancient-classical and medieval-Christian ideals of perfect social order, harmony, and cooperation. Here and there in those far past times, rare persons or groups had dreams of a total abolition of the competition, strife, conflict, power-lust, oppression, injustice, and justified rebellions, which were familiar and explained as results of selfish or unsocial individual, group, or class greeds or ambitions for exclusive ownership, control, and use of scarce economic resources. There were dreams of abolishing all that and achieving a complete social harmony, fraternity, and cooperation through collective ownership and management of all resources, and a program of cooperative labor in which all would contribute according to their abilities and share the fruits according to their needs. Suggestions of or toward this outlook can be found in scattered, minor, untypical parts of the literature of classical antiquity, and again in the records of some obscure, local, and ephemeral agitations within medieval Europe. Then in the time of the Renaissance, some individuals among the classical scholars and humanists, seeking to regain the moral wisdom of antiquity and apply it to the problems of the societies around them, wrote fictional portrayals of imaginary, ideal societies, as their way of indirectly criticizing the societies they lived in. The justly most famous of these works, Sir Thomas More's *Utopia,* which later gave its name or title to all such productions, was a truly socialistic tract by this great sixteenth century English scholar and statesman. Still, it was left for a few much later figures, in late eighteenth century France— figures there in the Enlightenment and in the French Revolution—to begin to give the socialist movement a real start and impetus and a more than ephemeral philosophy and active following, program, and tradition. If ancient-classical and Christian ideals of social harmony were the older sources of the socialist vision, an equally important, new source which now came into play was the ideal that pervaded the Enlightenment—the ideal of an applied-social-scientific, rational reorganization or reconstruction of all human societies that would scrap all irrational, merely traditional, institutions and practices and build a new social order scientifically designed to best fulfill all the needs of mankind.

Now the great majority of the exponents of that ideal in that epoch were, it is true, not socialists at all but liberals in the classical sense or advocates of the kind of world of extensive freedoms and opportunities for all individuals which is still the dominant American ideal. But along with the liberal majority, the whole group of the men of the Enlightenment included also a significant minority of more radical, socialist-and-anarchist thinkers or dreamers. In a sense their ultimate aims were quite similar to those of the liberals, but they had a widely different view of the amount and kind of institutional change that would be needed to attain their ends. The liberals saw as needed only abolition of some features of the traditional European "old regime" or social order. They wanted to abolish only such features as absolute or uncontrolled monarchy and aristocracy, all kinds of monopolies and special privileges for favored groups, and excessive restrictions of the freedoms, rights, and opportunities of most of the people as individuals. To be retained, with the revisions indicated, were the other familiar features of social life—private property and business enterprises, market competition, unequal incomes and wealth due to the unequal abilities and energies of different people, a division of the population into proprietors of business enterprises and hired workers in them, and governments with important though limited functions and coercive powers. But the liberals hoped that, as all individuals became secure in the enjoyment of their proper, extensive and equal freedoms, and "enlightened" by the advance and spread of knowledge and education, in general they would as free citizens learn to practice, in most cases voluntarily in the main, the rational conduct and cooperation which would progressively enhance and tend to maximize the economic and general welfare of each and of all of them. The radical socialist-and-anarchist philosophers, on the other hand, believed that for achievement of the perfect harmony among all and happiness of all of which they dreamed, a far more radical change of all institutions would be needed, away from all historic precedents. They envisioned as necessary in that sense, replacement of private by collective ownership of all means of production, that is, of all substantial wealth; collectively planned work and living, with assignments to all severally of the tasks and roles through which they could best contribute to the common welfare; and a division or distribution of the collective output or income, not by the market but by plan or agreement, on a more or less equal basis or according to needs or to sacrifices rather than abilities. Above all, there was to be payment only for productive, manual or mental work, not for rights to use private property or capital, of which there would be none; all persons would be workers only and get wages or salaries only, and there would be no upper and lower or richer and poorer classes, and no competition, strife, or conflict. With this socialist vision there was often combined the anarchist vision of an eventual disappearance of all coercive government and all coercion of some men by other men. For when all men learned to give up their private properties and acquisitive ambitions and join in cooperative work for the common good, and produce so much and share it so equally that all would have enough and be content; then all the conflicts making coercive governments necessary to maintain law and order would cease; cooperation among all would become entirely spontaneous, smooth, and harmonious; and governments would become unnecessary and be abolished.

The utopian dreams or visions of these two kinds which emerged out of the Enlightenment—both the moderately utopian liberal vision and the more radical and extremely utopian socialist-and-anarchist vision—both helped to inspire the high, enthusiastic fervor of the French Revolution and the wave of revolutionary efforts which swept over most of Europe in its wake. And the visionary ardor for reconstructing human societies on new, more humane, and "rational" lines continued on in many circles of intellectuals and reformers, all through the nineteenth century. In the earlier part of that century, France, not unnaturally in view of the turmoil of its then recent and current history, had a particularly numerous throng of active socialist thinkers and agitators; and Marx at an early point in his career went to France to confer with French socialists and in a great measure acquired from them the socialist vision which he retained as one part of the system of thought which he went on developing. But although Marx always acknowledged his debts to his socialist forerunners, he became rather severely critical of one important aspect of their way of thinking that he called "utopian." His own great aim came to be to create for use by all later socialists a new system of ideas and knowledge which he tried and claimed to make—and these are his words—scientific instead of utopian. Now it is important, if we are to understand Marxism, to understand clearly what Marx did and did not mean by this. He did not mean that the ideal vision of the earlier socialists, of the goal of their movement—the future, perfected socialist society—was utopian in the sense that it could never be realized in this world. In that sense, for those of us who do believe in the permanent impossibility of perfect harmony in real human societies, the vision of the socialist goal retained by

Marx himself was as utopian as that of his forerunners, for it was the same; and he never meant to change or criticize this part of their outlook. He condemned as utopian only their answer, which to his mind was no answer, to the question, how—through what process of social change, how brought about—the goal could and would be attained.

As true heirs of the Enlightenment, the pre-Marxian socialists were naïve rationalists who thought that by simply describing or blue-printing the new, ideal social order and way of life and proving its superior merits in logical arguments addressed to the public at large, they could in time convert mankind to their way of thinking and thus bring about adoption or enactment and realization of their vision. But Marx regarded this pure reliance on reasoned advocacy of the socialist ideal as unrealistic because he held that men in general can be led to understand, accept, and act in line with only those beliefs and ideals which are made convincing to them by their own real or tangible environments and circumstances and their own experiences, needs, and desires, and not simply by abstract, logical arguments. The states of men's minds, according to Marx, are so largely determined by their special circumstances and resulting interests that reasoning with them can do little or nothing to change their minds except insofar as those circumstances and interests are or come to be such as to make them receptive to the reasonings in question. The prosperous and comfortable people in the world's existing, nonsocialist societies would be and remain firm supporters of them, impervious to the ideas and arguments of the socialists, as long as they were prosperous and comfortable. Only in the mass of poor, miserable, and dissatisfied working people could the prophets of socialism hope to find a large, truly receptive audience. And even the working class would not as a whole become fully conscious of its real needs or interests and the real conditions of their satisfaction, and ready to fight or struggle effectively for their own salvation and against the opposition of the rich upholders of the existing order until, as predicted by Marx, the automatic evolution and degeneration of that order, capitalism, should bring about a further intensified misery of the working class which would goad it into revolutionary action, and a shrinkage and demoralization of the class of capitalists which would enable the revolution to succeed.

Marx, then, set out to make the views underlying the political methods employed by socialists realistic and effective instead of utopian in his sense, by giving them, in the place of their early, simple faith in the reasonableness of mankind and the unlimited power of reasoned argument or propaganda, the guidance of his new "science" of the history and prospects of mankind; that is, of the past and on-going, historical process of social change and the way to work effectively within and upon that, by anticipating inevitable changes and exploiting the opportunities afforded by them to bring about, or turn them into, desired changes in the direction of realization of the socialist ideal or vision. It is this so-called science, created by Marx, of the history and future of mankind as seen from the socialist angle of vision, that is the distinctive and main part of intellectual Marxism, and the part that we need above all to understand. It is of course by no means fully, truly scientific, but neither is it all pure nonsense, as most Americans are far too prone to suppose that it is. It is a vast and complicated mass of combined historical scholarship or knowledge and philosophical and social-scientific theories purporting to explain the past and predict the future; and a blend of much fantastic, visionary nonsense with many, largely true and often highly penetrating insights. As I said earlier, the basic, general philosophy of history involved in it was Marx's transformation and original, special development of the philosophy of history produced earlier by the great German philosopher Hegel, which Marx first learned or absorbed and began already to revise while he was still a young German university student, and thus even some years before he became definitely a socialist, or formed and matured his socialist outlook during his sojourn in France. Unless one begins with study of the Hegelian, it is hardly possible to understand the Marxist, philosophy of history; and although it is rash indeed on my part to try in the little time that I have here to do this, I must try to suggest a way of perhaps beginning to understand these two related, strange and difficult, intellectual creations.

It tends to be especially difficult for us Americans to understand the Hegelian and Marxist "historical" ways of thinking which try and claim to explain why and how all the past, great events or developments in all human history came about as they did and to forecast the on-going trend of the historical process far into the future; and which ground all their views on all social or public questions, in their visions of that entire process or the past and the future.

For such an outlook is extremely different from our own accustomed one, which retains much more of the character of the liberal outlook that was dominant in the eighteenth century Enlightenment—the classical, liberal vision of the essentially timeless or eternal, right or reasonable, general pattern of all human relations, institutions, and behavior, as something to be achieved and then preserved in its essentials through all subsequent historical or temporal change, which need alter only unessential details and should in fact bring an ever fuller or more perfect realization in practice of the ideal vision. History as such has never had any vast importance in or for our common or typical, American consciousness. We are a nation built by ex-Europeans turning their backs on their ancestral pasts and devoting themselves to building up here a new and better society and way of life in a new world; looking always forward and never backward, and conceiving the future as something to be freely shaped by living men, not controlled by continuing influences from the past. Also our largely migratory, relatively rootless people, living in at least relatively new, modern, and continually changing, man-made surroundings, learn about far past history, if at all, only in schools or from books and get little feeling of its reality or importance. But in Europe and all old societies, people live always surrounded by ancient monuments and all kinds of relics and reminders of their entire histories, and absorb the latter all their lives through their senses and imaginations, and are full of vivid, historical memories which largely control all their social views and expectations. Hence Marxism, with its claimed power to explain the past and present and foresee the future of all human societies, has a power of appealing or seeming cogent to the educated classes in all old societies that it lacks for us Americans. And we need to make the effort to understand this history-oriented way of thinking, so alien to our own, if we are to cope with all that is flowing from it in the world today.

Now the Marxist form and its parent, the Hegelian form, of this way of thinking have one additional, important, and not easily understood feature in common—the conception of the "dialectical" nature, form, and law of the historical process—and one point of contrast with and opposition to each other, involving Marx's philosophical position in favor of "materialism" as opposed to Hegel's "idealism." Let me touch on, first, the significance of the materialism *versus* idealism controversy, and then the notion of the dialectical movement of history. Philosophical idealism of the classical German and Hegelian kind was in essence the belief that the ultimate or fundamental and causally potent or creative reality in or behind not only all human life and history, but all nature or the universe as well, is not a material or physical but instead is a mental or spiritual reality—God, the Absolute, the world-spirit, or soul of all existence—a creative and rational, spiritual power which somehow generates or engenders all material or physical phenomena and all human deeds and tangible creations as approximate or imperfect realizations, embodiments, or manifestations to the human senses, of divine "ideas." Hegelian idealistic thought about everything, including human history and destiny, was a form or development of religious thought, which has deeply influenced much modern Protestant-Christian theology. And Marx was led to reject and oppose it and embrace its opposite, materialism, largely because he saw the connection of idealism with religion, and held a hostile view of the social role or function of all religion as a help to upper classes in maintaining antiquated social systems and as an impediment to all human progress, and thought of "materialism" on the other hand as the viewpoint of all progressive, modern science. I wish that I had time here to discuss the great questions which I must skirt around, about the antireligious and materialistic aspect of Marxism and Communism, which many people regard, I think mistakenly, as the main source of all that is evil in them. But I can speak here, further, only about idealism and materialism as applied in the two philosophies of history.

In that field, Hegel's idealism was the view that human thoughts are the important causes of all the human deeds and tangible creations and social systems that arise in the course of history; the spiritual-cultural side of history is the source of the rest of it; the evolution of the philosophies, sciences, and arts, or intellectual cultures, of human societies, controls the evolution of the societies themselves. And in this connection Marx's materialism was the opposing view, that all developments within the minds of men are in fact results of antecedent developments of their real societies, environments, and circumstances, which form their experiences and thus form their ideas, beliefs, and aspirations. Marx said that he found Hegel standing on his head and turned him over and set him upright on his feet. He further expressed the thesis of his "historical materialism" by saying that the state and the contents of man's consciousness do not determine his state of existence, but instead are determined by it. Yet that ideas and beliefs and systems of them, or social philosophies, or ideologies, to use the ugly word that we owe to Marx—that these, when they have been formed and widely embraced, do have or carry in themselves much history-making or world-changing power, Marx did not really deny. He only insisted that the rise and spread of every ideology itself is caused by the prior, independent evolution of the real societies, environments, and circumstances, and resulting experiences, desires, and attitudes of the masses of people concerned that dispose them to develop and believe that ideology; hence the latter is in every case potent only as the medium which transmits the power of each temporary state of an evolving, real, objective society to produce the next one. As we shall see in a moment, this view in its detailed development by Marx into a social-scientific theory became his "economic interpretation" of history, claiming to show that and how the economic development of societies causes and controls the development of their institutions, ideologies, and cultures. But before going on to speak further of this, I must try to explain, in a measure, the mysterious, Hegelian-and-Marxian idea of the dialectical, historical process.

To me it seems a little less difficult to understand this idea in its original, Hegelian, idealistic form than in its altered, Marxian, materialistic form, so I start with the former. The word "dialectics" in its original use and meaning, in ancient

Greek thought, referred to the kind of intellectual process that goes on in a discussion or argument between the exponents of two opposite theses or points of view, who in the course of their discussion mutually enlighten and learn from each other, and modify their initial positions and combine their insights, until they reach agreement on a new, third position which is self-consistent but nearer to the whole truth on the subject than was either initial position because it unites the partial truths that were in both of them. And as the old Greek dialecticians knew, in the ever on-going course of discussion or joint inquiry, each new "synthesis" of the contributions arising from an original "thesis" and the "antithesis" or counter-thesis responsive to that could in turn become a new thesis evocative of a new antithesis, and the next round of the debate could then lead on to a new and still higher, more inclusive synthesis—and so on. Now Hegel regarded the history of philosophy and, more broadly, that of all intellectual culture as a progressive process proceeding in that way; and, with his "idealistic" belief that the history of thought is the creative part of all history, which controls the rest of it, Hegel formed his philosophy of history on the model of his idea of the "dialectical" history or progress of philosophy. Particular societies in particular areas and epochs—in modern times, nations, and in earlier times their nearest equivalents—have developed civilizations pervaded and inspired by particular patterns of ideas, beliefs, and ideals, or distinctive visions of all existence and all values. And the vision, philosophy, ideology, or thesis dominant for a time in the culture of each society has tended while it prevailed to mould that society into an approximate realization or embodiment of itself. But contrasting societies evolving and shaped by opposed or warring ideologies have come into contact and conflict with each other and through their conflicts have influenced and modified each other's systems of ideas and practices and produced syntheses of their initially conflicting, partial wisdoms into fuller and truer wisdoms. The conflicts and mergers of diverse, one-sided civilizations, leading on to new conflicts and new mergers, have been making up a progress of all civilization toward an eventual, future, perfect, world-civilization which will have and realize the complete, harmonious, true vision of all ideal reality.

But now let me add to that first, partial explanation of Hegel's theory, a new and different one. To do this I must first refer to an older outlook, common among philosophers before Hegel's time, that may be called "metaphysical rationalism"—the belief that rational or logical consistency or harmony obtains not only among all truths but also among all realities; that the real world or universe is throughout an internally consistent, rational, harmonious system. Now to make that assumption about the actual world as it already, overtly is at any time would make it very difficult to explain why anything would ever change through time; there would be every reason to expect a perfectly consistent, harmonious world to be stable, static, fixed, or immutable through time. In point of fact those earlier philosophers, before Hegel, who did believe in the necessity of harmony not only among all true thoughts but also among all their real objects or all the parts of the real universe, did not, when they made this view itself clear and self-consistent, identify or treat as one the two notions of "reality" and "actuality." Instead they meant by the real, the ideal world, and thought of the actual world at any time as an only approximate or imperfect materialization of ideal "reality." This was Hegel's position too, and the revision that he made of the older view about logic and the real world was only a clarification. But there had been confused tendencies to think of even the actual world as self-consistent, rational, and harmonious, and these had hampered the growth of understanding or any adequate conceptions of temporal change, process, history, or evolution. Hegel's innovation was to insist that while "reality" in the sense of the ideal world—the world as it ought to be and must eventually become, the *goal* of evolution or the historical process—is indeed consistent, rational, harmonious; the process itself or the changing, actual world is full of, and propelled along through its changes by, internal conflicts or "contradictions," which successively develop and resolve themselves in the "dialectical" way. History is a progress toward eventual realization of the ideal harmony, through a series of inevitable and fruitful conflicts. The incompatibilities of or among the different, temporary parts of the actual, temporal world make it unstable, or unable to endure as it is, and compel or produce the changes logically required to eliminate or resolve the incompatibilities and bring into existence, in the end, the entirely harmonious world which alone will be stable or enduring.

Hegel's emphasis in developing his theory of the "dia-

lectical," evolutionary process in human history was upon
the conflicts of different national civilizations and the "syntheses" of them achieved, often, through wars and conquests
and the exchanges of influence between the conquering and
conquered nations. He was a Prussian patriot, deeply interested in what he saw in his time as the conflict and the
coming, necessary synthesis of Prussian-German *Kultur* and
the more modern and more Western or British and French
liberalism of the Enlightenment. But while for Hegel, the
next phase, at least, of the advance toward the final harmony
was to be the realization of his ideal of a half-liberalized
Prussia; for Marx, with his in most respects entirely different
outlook, the final harmony was to be realized through or
in world-wide socialism. And for Marx the important, conflicting entities were not nations but the upper and lower,
or oppressing and oppressed, social classes within all nations.
Also for him the conflicts and syntheses of ideologies—the
philosophies or outlooks evolved by the warring classes to
express and implement their class-interests—were only reflections of the real, material conflicts inherent in the incom-
patible, objective situations and imperative needs of the
classes within their evolving, actual societies. But to get more
light on Marx's theory of the historical process we must now
move on, beyond his revision of Hegel's philosophy into his
alleged social and economic science; and consider in this
area, first, his economic interpretation of history and, as
closely connected with that, his theory of the class struggles
through which the changes of economic systems and conditions have caused all broader social and cultural changes.

There is a common, erroneous idea that the Marxist "economic interpretation of history" is or means the theory that the economic motive, so-called, or the human desire or greed for wealth or economic gains, underlies and causes all that human beings think, feel, do, or create. This cynical theory that human nature is dominated by the profit motive was not Marx's theory at all. In his view, the peculiar, excessive development and strength of that motive in the members of the capitalist class in the part or period of history dominated by the special, transitory, capitalist system was to be regarded as an aberration, or a product and part of capitalism only and not a universal and permanent, inherent trait of "human nature"; and his economic interpretation of history was meant to explain all history, not the capitalist part of it alone, hence the basic reference is to something else, not this economic motive. His basic idea in this connection was in fact that the objective economic conditions, situations, or circumstances in which people live so strongly affect or color all of their experiences, thoughts, and desires or motives as to play the main role in forming their outlooks, characters, and conduct. The ancient, Greek and Roman, slave-owning gentries and their slaves; medieval, feudal lords, and peasants; and modern, factory-owning business men and hired factory-workers—all, in their times, societies, and classes, have been made into the different kinds of people they have been—caused to think, feel, and behave as they did or do—mainly by the effects upon them of the economic or material environments, circumstances, and conditions of their lives. And within the historical process,

Marx held, a largely autonomous evolution of the techniques, methods, and organizations of economic activities and production is continually changing the roles, relations, and situations of the economic classes and the conditions of life for their members, and thus changing them as people and causing them to change their beliefs and actions and all parts of their societies and cultures. In the available time I cannot say more either in further explanation of this general theory or in discription of the elaborations of it by Marx and his followers and of their efforts to support it with factual, historical evidence, or in expression of the severely critical comments I would like to make on it. I must turn to the third and final part of Marx's system as a whole—his economic theory or analysis, not of all history but of the capitalist part of it—his theory of the structure, working, inner conflicts and dilemmas, and evolution and impending doom of the modern Western economic system, industrial capitalism, and the social order and civilization viewed by him as dependent on it; and his prophecy of the future system, socialism, that would happily replace it.

Whatever estimates may be made of Marx's intellectual work in his roles as philosopher, sociologist, and historian, he was I think beyond doubt an economist of considerable stature although by no means without his failings and errors in that field. He was a keen, able, and industrious scholar and investigator, and attained a wide and deep knowledge both of the works of most other economists of his own and earlier times, and of the real economic world around him in his time. And he largely mastered and accepted, made his own, and used and built upon or added to, the insights of his great forerunners in the study of economics, Adam Smith, Ricardo, and others, although he changed some of their ideas or doctrines, in some cases for the worse, to fit them into his own system. His bias, of course, was of a kind opposite to that which may in a measure be justly charged against Adam Smith and the entire, main, orthodox line of great nineteenth century economists, who as liberals in the classical sense in their social-and-moral philosophies or outlooks, tended to be friendly or favorable to the liberal or free and competitive form of capitalism or the business economy. Marx as a radical, revolutionary socialist was a bitterly hostile, adverse critic of that economic system, and therefore constructed as compared with theirs a rather different, theoretical picture of its "natural" working and development. But I think his hostile and their favorable bias led mainly to different insights and discoveries, and different blind spots or limitations of insight, and made his analysis of the real system and its functioning and prospects in some ways complementary to theirs. The liberal, "orthodox" economists far excelled him in discerning, analyzing, and describing the better possibilities or best potential functioning of the business economy; but he excelled them in discerning, analyzing, and describing its defects or flaws and possible and frequent internal maladjustments and malfunctionings, and capacities to go wrong and make serious trouble for itself. With his extreme bias against the system and desire to prove it a thing so evil that it must inevitably destroy itself, he exaggerated all its flaws and discordant tendencies and falsely claimed to prove that they were inherent, incurable, and bound to grow worse and destroy the system and open the way to the bright future of socialism. But I think we can, without accepting any of his nonsense of that kind, learn much from his work in economics which can improve our own realistic understanding of the business economy.

Being framed within the wider context of his theory of all human history or social evolution, Marx's system of theory about the economics of capitalism or the business economy endeavored to explain not only its current operation or functioning in his time, but also and above all its past and current and prospective evolution as an unstable or dynamic, growing, and changing system. His prophecies about its fate were biased and in essential parts have been and are being disproved by actual events, but there was much truth in his vision of its dynamic, evolving nature, which few other economists have grasped and analyzed as well as he did. More clearly than anyone else, before his time at least, he saw this fact about capitalism as an economic system: that by its nature it is bound or at least strongly tends to be not a static, fixed, immutable but a very dynamic, growing or expanding, and perpetually self-changing and world-changing affair. To explain this fact, Marx offered a not uninstructive comparison or contrast of capitalism with a different, simpler, half historic or precapitalist and half imaginary or hypothetical kind of commercial or exchange economy, which he called simple commodity production. In the latter system, there would be a division of labor, or specialized producers of different products, and private properties and enterprises in a sense, and markets for the selling and buying of the different products, but the crucial feature of capitalism as conceived by Marx would be absent; that is, there would be no separate class of owners or proprietors, investors, and employers, and no dependent class of hired workers owning only their abilities to work. All members of this economic society would be self-employed workers or producers, owning their own premises, tools, materials, and products, and simply earning their livings by producing goods to sell to each other for the money they would severally use to buy from each other all that they needed to live on. In this simple system, said Marx, the formula describing the typical pair of market transactions continually repeated by each individual as a producer and consumer would be C-M-C; one would sell his commodity or product, C, for money, and spend the money in buying other products, C again, in total value equal to that of his own output and sales. And the gain or advantage would lie simply in getting the other goods you want more urgently, or which have more utility or value-in-use for you than the goods you sold in order to be able to buy them. No physical, quantitative increase of your wealth over time would be needed in this system to give meaning, point, or purpose to economic activities. But in the capitalist system, the investing, owning, and labor-employing capitalist starts with a sum of money to invest at or for a profit, and the formula that describes the sequence of his transactions is M-C-M', where the M' needs to be bigger than the M to make it all worth while. The capitalist invests his money, M, in equipping and hiring workers to produce an output, C, which he aims to sell for M′, more money than he started with. And Marx imputed to all typical capitalists or business men a very powerful urge or drive toward gaining the largest possible profits, and then reinvesting most of those profits as additions to their amounts of capital in order to get still larger profit-incomes, and so on. And he held that the resulting, snow-balling accumulation, growth, or expansion of the mass of capital in the system, and the constant and growing need or pressure to keep on finding or creating ever new, profitable investment opportunities or outlets, and markets for more and more new products, accounted for the inherent tendency of the capitalist system to grow and change or evolve in the course of time.

Moreover, Marx recognized a good or beneficial side to that, for mankind, at least through the early, progressive phase of the life-cycle that he thought would be that of the capitalist system. Though he hated capitalism as compared with his vision of the socialist heaven-on-earth that would some day replace it, he could still praise capitalism as compared with older or earlier and worse systems in past human history—the slave-economy of antiquity and the feudal system of the Middle Ages. There is in *The Communist Manifesto,* the famous first small book by Marx and Engels setting forth the gist of Marx's vision of the history and destiny of mankind, a famous passage that is often called his "hymn of praise" to capitalism and might have been written by any Rotarian. There he says that in a few generations of

modern European history the *bourgeoisie* or capitalist class
has brought about a greater advance of economic production
and wealth than had been achieved in all previous human
history, and has thus made possible a great growth of population, and built up cities, drawing masses of people out of
rural stagnation into urban civilization and progress. Yet
this giving of credit to the profit-gaining and accumulating
and investing and enterprising capitalists, for economic
progress or rising productivity, was hardly consistent with
his central economic doctrine, that all profits and property-
incomes result entirely from exploitation or underpayment
of hired workers, who alone produce or create all of the
"value" of all output but get only bare or meager living
wages, while all of the surplus of their total output over
what they need to keep them alive and working goes into
the profit, interest, and rent incomes of their capitalist masters, the owners of all "means of production." Marx's capitalists seem to be at once, through their investing and
enterprising activities, great developers or increasers of the
productivity of industry and labor, and yet mere parasites
on the working class, which alone is productive but is forced
to surrender a great part of its output to its capitalist masters.
I cannot here discuss the mysteries and follies of the Marxist
"labor theory of value," so called, and the connected "theory
of surplus value" or all capitalist incomes. But I must say a
word about the third leg of this tripod, Marx's theory or
doctrine as to how and at what level the real wages of hired
labor are determined in the capitalist system. The theory
that real wages tend to be only barely sufficient to support

or maintain an adequate labor force in the economy at a fixed, low standard of living, was already a part of the Ricardian, classical theory of economics which Marx knew well and largely accepted, used, and built upon. But in the classical form, this pessimistic theory about wages explained the alleged tendency with the aid of the Malthusian theory of population growth and pressure, which Marx scornfully rejected, calling it a "libel on the human race." According to Marx, wages under capitalism tend to the bare subsistence level, not because the workers multiply or breed too fast whenever they prosper at all and thus create or maintain the chronic oversupply of labor which depresses wages; but because the capitalists, striving to maintain a high rate of profit despite the constant increase of the supply of capital and supplies of all goods on the markets, are continually further mechanizing all production to increase its efficiency and decrease their costs, or introducing more and more new labor-saving inventions or machines, which displace workers from their jobs into what he called "the reserve army of the unemployed." He granted that such technological unemployment tended to be temporary for particular workers as the lowering of costs would increase total consumption and production over time, and the displaced workers would eventually find new jobs in the expanding economy. But while the workers made superfluous in their old employments by new labor-saving machines were being reabsorbed elsewhere into the active labor force, new mechanizations would be continually displacing other workers, and the "reserve army" would always exist and by the competition of its members for the jobs of employed workers hold wages down. Now there is a process of this kind, but there is no reason for it to work this strongly or force and hold wages in general down to a bare subsistence level, and the predictions of Marx in this matter have long since been disproved by actual events. He actually predicted even, in the later part of the life-history of capitalism, a progressive worsening of the situation for the working class, an intensification of its poverty and misery, but in fact there has been and continued to be a pronounced, rising trend of the level of real wages in all progressive capitalist countries.

For Marx's general theory and forecast, however, of the evolution of dynamic capitalism, he really needed only, not his false theory that it would forever hold wages down to a bare subsistence level, but only his valid point, that the total value of the total output of the economy would normally exceed the total wages-bill or wage-income of the hired laboring class, and the surplus of the value of output over the cost of producing it would go into profits and property-incomes and through them in large part into new investments, increasing the volume of capital and leading to growth and change in the economy. But a further, important part of his general theory of that process of growth and change was about its fluctuating course and character, or what more modern economists have called the recurring "business cycle" of alternating prosperities or booms and depressions, and Marx called the crisis that would return every ten years or so in the life-history of capitalism. These have been real, serious, and very complex affairs, and economists have long been learning more and more about them but still don't fully understand and agree on either the full, true explanation of them or how to cure or cope with them. And Marx achieved no full, unified, and fully illuminating analysis of them but was among the first, among economists, to begin to understand them as natural episodes in the functioning and development of the unstable, dynamic, business system. In a way, whereas most efforts to explain the business cycle have been mainly efforts to explain depressions—assuming prosperity or full employment and good incomes for all as the normal state of the economy, and trying to explain the recurrent departures from that— for Marx with his general view of the system as a wretched one, the chief problem one may say was to explain prosperities. He envisaged the majority of the people as never getting more than bare livings, hence never able to afford to buy and consume very much; and the rich minority of capitalists as so eager to accumulate and reinvest their profits that they would not be lavish consumers either; but the continual growth of the system's capital and producing power would thus tend to exceed the growth of its consuming power and glut all the markets or produce chronic depression. Prosperities would occur, in the Marxist picture, only in the periods of preparatory expansion of plant-capacity, for future production of more consumers' goods, with new, improved machines and methods and thus at lower expected costs. Such expansions, not immediately yielding any great increases of the current output of consumers' goods, but bringing a temporary, near approach

to full employment, better wages for the workers tempo-
rarily, and good profits for all the capitalists selling new
machines, materials, and so on, to the other capitalists investing eagerly in them in the expectation of good future
profits for themselves from future sales to ultimate consumers—in short, a period of prosperity. But the strong
demand for labor and materials and machines would bid
up costs and cut down the prospective profits on further,
new investments; and the emergence in time of a new flood
of consumers' goods would bring to light the inadequacy
of the system's consuming power, and again glut the markets and bring on a depression. This is not all Marx had to offer nor the most surely valid part of what he had to offer, to
explain the cycle or the recurring crises, but I think I have
not unfairly summarized a characteristic part of his theory
of the matter. There is one more point to add in describing
his view about crises—he was confident that as new ones
came along they would get worse or increasingly severe,
and the final one would be the utter breakdown of the
system that would ignite the revolution and insure its triumph. It is not surprising that the great depression of the
nineteen thirties, which was or seemed the worst one yet
and so bad that it might be the final breakdown, gave intellectual Marxism at that time a tremendous boost or
growth of influence in our Western world. But there is no
conclusive evidence of an historic trend to ever increasingly
severe business depressions, and no reason, today, to doubt
that Western business men and working men and governments can and will learn to master, control, and moderate

these fluctuations and enable capitalism to endure and progressively correct its faults and improve its performance for the economic welfare of all the people.

The one part of Marx's theory of evolving capitalism which I have not touched on at all was his theory that along with its fluctuating growth or expansion it would undergo a structural change, from the early, competitive capitalism of very many, small or moderate-sized, competing enterprises to a latter day monopoly capitalism dominated by a few giant firms and financial dynasties. Competition among business firms would destroy itself, as the few winners would destroy or absorb the many losers in the game, and the growth of the mass of capital in the system would be accompanied by a concentration of the ownership or control of nearly all of it in the hands of a diminishing number of increasingly rich men and groups of them. In part this prophecy of Marx rested on his over-simple and exaggerated notion of the economy or efficiency of bigness in firms—his assumption that there was no limit to the rule that the bigger the firm, the more efficient it could be, so that growth of the average size and reduction of the number of successful firms would be the natural law of business development. We know now that this matter is not so simple; bigness has advantages in many fields up to some point, but there seem to be limits, though not rigidly fixed ones; and smaller enterprises in many fields continue to be numerous and flourishing. Whether there is a trend away from competition of the old, classical kind toward increasing prevalence and power of monopolies within the economy is still uncertain.

The biggest firms are bigger than any that existed fifty or a hundred years ago, but the market areas throughout which firms are in competition with each other are also much bigger than they were then, and a firm's monopoly power depends on not its absolute size but its size relative to that of its market. Marx showed foresight in predicting the growth of modern big business but overshot the mark in predicting that the giants would become so big and few and all-controlling that the altered system, consisting merely of them and their few rich owners and the vast mass of starving and rebellious workers, would be ripe for sure and easy transformation into the socialist or Communist system.

The false vision of a latter day monopoly capitalism, of a few giant firms and cartels bestriding the earth and leaving no room for smaller enterprises, has been further developed by the modern disciples of Marx into the basis of their theory of what they call capitalist imperialisms,—the control of the underdeveloped countries of the world by and for the great capitalists in the advanced or fully evolved, capitalist countries. In my next lecture, I shall discuss this in its place in what the Communists of today have made out of Marxism, as the basis of their mental pictures of the world of today and their expectations, aims, and policies. I have also not discussed or mentioned the small part of Marx's own system of thought which went beyond his analysis of evolving capitalism and prediction of its doom and dealt, only briefly and vaguely, with the question how the new, glorious, socialist system was to be constructed, organized, operated, and developed after the revolution. But this too can be left over for the next lecture, since Marx in fact said so little about this that what his modern Communist disciples have said and are doing is the main thing in this area that is worth discussing. He spoke of a destruction, by the victorious working class in its revolution, of the states and governments which he regarded as, in all capitalist countries no matter how democratic their nominal, political systems might be, really mere executive committees of the capitalist class; and the creation by the revolting workers of a temporary state and government of a new kind, the dictatorship of the proletariat, which would build and perfect the new socialist economic system and get it working perfectly and then go out of existence or wither away, leaving just the workers to cooperate in perfect freedom, for their common welfare, under no governmental or other coercion or control. But the dream of perfect order, harmony, and cooperation, unmarred by any dissents and conflicts, has not unnaturally swallowed up the dream of perfect individual freedom and become a recipe for total despotism, since among free men there are bound to be conflicts if they are not suppressed. The element of utopianism in the thought of Marx was its greatest weakness, and the professed builders of his utopia are making it a hell.

Chapter III ~ AMERICAN LIBERALISM *Versus* COMMUNISM IN THE WORLD TODAY

My theme tonight is concerned with Communism as a development of Marxism, and the issues at stake in our struggle with it. Now at the outset of this discussion it is important to emphasize a peculiar feature that is common to the by no means identical Marxisms of Marx himself and the present day Communists. I refer to the fact that in all intellectual Marxism, what is mainly emphasized and elaborated is not any set of ideals or normative principles or any program or prescriptions for construction, operation, and development of Marxian-socialist or Communist forms or systems of economy, society, and government; but only a supposedly positive or scientific theory of the past and current and prospective, on-going, historical process of social change or evolution of all human societies, toward a predestined, eventual, future realization of an ideal vision that remains largely unspecified or unformulated; and a set of prescriptions of the supposedly necessary or required, effective strategy and tactics to be used by the party or movement in playing its role as the instrument of history or destiny, in bringing about the inevitable and desired consummation of that process. Marxist thought has never offered or contained an at all detailed or clear blueprint of the goal—the ideal socialist society; but has been preoccupied with explaining the past and predicting the future course of world history, analyzing the faults and malfunctionings and resulting instabilities and inevitable changes of all pre-socialist systems and especially of capitalism, and charting the road to the socialist goal, and the methods to be used in the struggle to attain it. Now our American and Western liberalism is primarily a conception of the ethics or ethical principles that should be observed or carried out within and among all societies and social movements; and yet in its own way it also is concerned less with final ends or goals than with the kinds of methods which should and others which should not be used in the efforts of men and groups to attain whatever ends they decide to seek. And the Marxist and especially the modern Communist methods are decidedly unethical, by liberal standards.

Thus, I think, the main issues, or great moral issues, in our struggle with the Communists, pertain much less to the relative merits of capitalism and socialism than to the question of ethical and unethical ways of working to make either one prevail. It is true, of course, however, that the kind of realized, so-called socialist system—the actual system, institutions, and domestic and foreign policies brought into being and effect in the countries now ruled by Communist parties—is in every case a system made up of the evil results of the evil methods employed to build, operate, develop, and preserve it, and so must as a system fall under the con-

demnation of the same ethical principles which condemn
those methods. Whatever an ideal socialism may be in
theory, the actual socialism or so-called socialism or actual
system that is being developed and operated by these fanatical, ruthless, and unscrupulous revolutionists in all the
countries they control is naturally, in consequence of their
methods, a brutal and treacherous, inhuman affair of authoritarian police states which enslave and exploit the main
masses or majorities in their own populations, and strive to
expand their power and system in the world by fomenting
and controlling revolutions, in other countries wherever
they can; and where they succeed they bring about great
changes, in some ways progressive, in some cases, for the
peoples concerned.

Yet although we must morally condemn, along with the
methods of the Communists, the kind of realized socialism,
if that is the right name for it, which results from and em-
bodies their methods, I think the question whether all socialism is to be condemned is a different question. The
world has long contained, since a time long before there
were any Communists in the modern sense, and it still con-
tains today, large numbers of gentle, moderate, and more or
less rational, idealistic socialists of other, quite different
kinds, whose aims *and* methods of working to attain them
may be described as entirely civilized, humane, and liberal.
Most English socialists, Scandinavian socialists, and other
such groups of decidedly non- and anti-Communist and
either entirely or largely non-Marxian or only nominally
Marxian socialists, are in this category. As a rule they are

as deeply devoted as are any of us to liberal democracy and liberal ideals or principles of freedom and justice for all men, and sincerely intend to see that these shall be, and believe that they can be, fully preserved and even much more fully realized in the socialist societies they are working to achieve or create than they are or can be in any societies with capitalistic or private enterprise economic systems. I am not saying at all that I personally agree, for I do not agree, with these, in purpose and conviction, democratic and liberal socialists. I am myself a defender of liberal capitalism or the economic system of largely free, private enterprises, and competitive markets, and I think it is much more surely in harmony with liberalism and democracy than any socialism can be in practice. In fact I very gravely doubt the long-run compatibility of any complete or all-out socialism —collective or public ownership and control of entire, national economies or substantially all economic resources— with real democracy and individual liberty of any kind. For in practice this would surely mean control of substantially all wealth at every current time by the existing government, and no real chance for the opposition or any opposition party or group to have the support of any independent economic resources. But the in spirit liberal and democratic socialists think they can solve this problem and intend to solve it, and I think their ideals and characters generally are such that if and as they fail to solve it, as I think they will, they will give up the goal of complete socialism rather than give up liberalism and democracy. In fact I think they are well on the way to doing that already and watering down their socialism into a limited welfare-state-ism very similar to the revised or modified liberalism that is generally known by the latter name today in this country. At this point, however, I want above all to say that among the different countries in the free world of today there must be mutual toleration of each other's disagreeing views on these matters, and differing forms of mixed economies or systems in the range between the extremes of old fashioned, *laissez faire* capitalism and complete socialism in the classical sense of that word. And I think such tolerance and disagreement can be entirely consistent with complete agreement, throughout the free world, in moral opposition to the Communist methods and *regimes.*

Without any abatement, however, of my condemnation of those methods and *regimes,* tonight I want above all, if I can, to contribute something to our understanding of their sources, and the sources of the strong appeal of Communism to the minds of millions of people, in the Marxist vision or philosophy as developed with some changes from that of Marx himself, by the modern Communists. I think we can get some light on all this by reviewing the evolution of modern Communist thought from that of Marx, which I surveyed in my last previous lecture, and examining both some of the elements which derive from Marx, and others which have grown out of other sources. Let us start by getting into our minds again the basic Marxist idea: that every non-socialist human society necessarily undergoes throughout its history a process of evolution or continual change of all aspects of its structure and functioning; an evolution that supposedly is caused by inevitable, inner conflicts between the oppressing and oppressed social classes within the society, and proceeds toward a final resolution of those conflicts or attainment of a final harmony—reorganization of the society into a socialist one, marked by a perfect, spontaneous cooperation of or among all its members as free and equal comrades, no longer divided into upper and lower classes, and all devotedly working for the common good or welfare of all. Further, according to Marxism, the deeper, underlying cause of the entire evolution to that idyllic outcome—the deeper cause of the evolution and of the class-struggles which immediately cause it—is technological and economic progress or the changing and improving methods and rising productivity of the society's processes of production of all useful, material goods. The characters, activities, outlooks, and relations of the social classes are, it is held, first results of and then, as Marx said, fetters upon or impediments to technological and economic progress or the series of industrial revolutions which recurrently transform the economy and society. Each general way of producing material goods, or set of techniques employed in producing them, requires and brings about a suitably related organization of the society and the relations of or among its members; a class of productive workers with a certain status, and a class of owners of the main resources or forms of wealth and rulers of the economy and society, using the power based on their wealth to control everyone else and everything in their class-interest. Further, continuing technological and economic progress creates needs for and becomes dependent on new social or institutional changes; but the dominant class, fearing loss of its power, resists or works to prevent these, and by so doing increasingly hampers or impedes the on-going technological and economic progress. Finally, the increasingly severe exploitation, by the dominant class, of the class or classes below it in the social scale, drives it or them into revolutionary action; and the increasingly bad or serious malfunctioning of the conflict-ridden economic system dooms it, or insures the success of the revolution and the creation of a new and better economic and social system, adapted to and able to facilitate the current phase of technological and economic progress. Historic and on-going social change, in other words, is envisaged in Marxist thought as mainly, through long intervals, spontaneous and gradual, evolutionary change, but with violent revolutions at long intervals, at the widely separated, crucial turning points, playing their essential roles. The liberal-democratic revolutions of the late eighteenth and early nineteenth century were, according to Marx, the necessary completions of the evolution from medieval feudalism to modern capitalism. And in his forward vision it was to be the mission of the coming, inevitable, and final, socialist or workers' revolution to complete the evolution of capitalism into socialism and create the latter as an ideal, classless, egalitarian, and conflict-free or entirely harmonious, cooperative form of society. In this final utopia when it should be or become perfected, all coercive government, a thing made necessary in all earlier social systems at bottom only by class-conflicts, would become needless and whither away; the Marxist utopia is to combine realized socialism and anarchism or a perfect, voluntary cooperation among all and no coercive government or coercive control of anyone by anyone. But during the transition immediately following the initial, victorious, workers' revolution, or while the new system is still being constructed and developed, there must be a temporary, new form of perhaps highly coercive government, superseding the old, capitalist-dominated governments—a "dictatorship" of or by the organized working class or proletariat, to suppress and destroy the last remnants of the *bourgeois* spirit of private greediness and reeducate the entire population to make it one of wisely and happily cooperating workers.

Now, having thus summarized the central doctrines of Marx, let me go on to discuss the extent, and the limits of the extent, to which those doctrines may be held to account for the evil tendencies in modern Communism. Here I think much depends or turns on the matter of relative degrees of stress on the evolutionary and revolutionary parts of the Marxist vision. Marx himself expected that the transformations of all capitalist into socialist economies and societies would come about mainly through a long, largely peaceful, and gradual, spontaneous evolution, and that the culminating, violent revolutions and immediately resulting, working-class dictatorships, which probably would be necessary in most countries when each one reached that advanced stage of its evolution through and beyond the phase of industrial capitalism, would be rather brief, mild, and minor affairs, playing their minor though essential roles.

Marx even thought and said that perhaps a few countries—
and he mentioned England as one—might escape the phase
of violent revolution and the working-class dictatorship entirely or achieve the final transformations of their capitalist
into socialist systems by a wholly peaceful or nonviolent,
evolutionary process. Only where the capitalists would remain unyielding to the last, or refuse to give up their wealth
and power until defeated in a violent struggle, would there
be such a struggle. And although Marx expected this to
occur in most cases or countries, he thought it could, should,
and would be a limited affair if the workers and socialists
themselves would adhere to the right course or path, which
he advocated. Having himself witnessed the generally un-
successful or abortive and repressed, European revolutions
of 1848, Marx continually preached to his followers against
premature attempts to carry out the socialist revolution, and
counseled patient waiting for the automatic evolution of
the capitalist system to do its full work, which eventually
would make the revolution at once truly inevitable, unavoid-
able, or necessary and certain to succeed quickly and easily.
In short, Marx advocated revolutions only in the fullness
of time, in the favorable situations which he thought the
evolutionary process, if let alone long enough, would
everywhere create. In the meantime, the working class and
its leaders in all countries were to organize and prepare for
the eventual, great day and be ready to seize and utilize
the right moment or opportunity; but they must wait
patiently for that to come, and if they would do so, they
would then need only to finish the work already almost

completely done for them by the evolution of capitalism itself to the point of ripeness for easy transformation into socialism.

As time and change went on, however, after the time of Marx, it proved to be a very difficult, harassing business for the German and central European, Marxian socialist or social-democratic parties to continue to follow the advice of Marx. Political parties must have programs of immediate action, promising to yield immediate benefits to their voting members and adherents if they are to retain the latter and increase their numbers. While those socialist parties which were and long remained at least nominally Marxist, always did have such programs, with the blessing of Marx up to a point, still it was very difficult, as long as they were entirely faithful to the doctrines of Marx, to make their programs of immediate action—to be carried out while waiting for the distant future, "revolutionary situation" to arrive—at once consistent with the doctrines of Marx and politically adequate. The only big, important change of conditions for the better, for the working class, could not be expected or achieved, according to their creed, until that rather remote future time when the long evolution and deterioration of capitalism should have run its full course, and made it possible to carry out their main, ultimate, or long-run program, that is, the revolution and the subsequent construction of the socialist society. In the meantime, only minor things could be done, and there was danger of doing or advocating the wrong things. Not only was substantial improvement of the lot of the working class within capitalism held to be impossible; their master had taught also that in the course of the evolution of capitalism, the lot of the workers was bound to, and needed to, get worse and worse to the point of filling or firing them all with enough revolutionary spirit to insure the eventual occurrence and success of the revolution, which alone would lead to their salvation. And if reforms that would alleviate the hardships of the workers were carried out within capitalistic states, there was danger that their effects would be to decrease the militancy or increase the relative contentment of the workers and bolster up the capitalist system and prolong its life and further postpone the future, real or great improvement.

A growing sense of that dilemma, and the pressing political need to escape from it, was one factor that helped to produce in those old, late nineteenth and very early twentieth century Marxian-socialist, but not in the modern sense Communist, parties in central, southern, northern, and western Europe a "rightward" trend of their main tendencies of feeling and practice, away from strict, real adherence to their Marxism, and toward, in real effect, practical agreement with the always mainly non-Marxian, Fabian, English brand of socialism. But another, concurrent factor which also helped to produce that trend was a growing awareness of the fact that the actual evolution of maturing capitalism in those countries was not in all respects bearing out the predictions of Marx. A growing, relative concentration or centralization of wealth and power in a smaller number of larger and stronger business enterprises, units, or organizations, which Marx had predicted, was indeed occurring. But this development appeared to many observers, including many formerly Marxian socialists, to be making each national and the Western world's economic system not weaker but stronger; not more unstable but more stable or less subject to the threat of increasingly severe business depressions; and more or increasingly able and disposed to gradually improve the real wages and working and living conditions of the workers and accept or tolerate new, multiplying, small reforms of public and prevailing, private business policies, all tending to enhance the welfare and contentment of the mass of working people, and remove the prospect of impending revolution. On the basis, then, of both that new assessment of the current, actual evolution of capitalism, and the feeling of the practical, political value of working mainly and without inhibitions for all the moderate steps or measures of reform that were becoming increasingly feasible; there grew up within those Marxian-socialist parties the "revisionist" movement which advocated open abandonment of the doctrines of Marx, and conversion of the parties that had borne his banner into non-revolutionary or moderate, reformist parties, hoping to realize socialism in the long run by gradually reforming capitalism. In the doctrinal or propaganda battles that ensued, it is true, the revisionists were defeated, nominally, and the professedly orthodox Marxists remained in control of the party organizations. But in real effect, as shown in the subsequent, prevailing, practical attitudes and behavior of the parties,

revisionism won; the continuing, professed allegiance to
Marxism became only lip-service, and the parties moved
increasingly along the paths of moderate, gradual reform
through successful, current, political action.

That, broadly, is what happened in the Western world,
very generally, in the interval between the lifetime of
Marx and the occurrence in 1917 of the Russian revolution
in which Lenin and his Bolsheviki seized power in Russia
and began the creation of the now very formidable Communist system of theory and practice with which we are
confronted today. In one vital respect, the entire development since then, of and in the now Communist countries,
has been wholly contrary to Marx's predictions and advice,
but understandable I think in the light of facts about economic and social evolution which he did not know and
therefore did not take into account. According to Marx's
expectations and advice the first successful workers' socialist revolutions were to occur in the already, previously,
most advanced or fully developed, capitalist, industrial
countries—England, western Europe, and the United
States; and each country in the world would and should
undergo the revolution and move from the capitalist into
the socialist camp only after going through, itself, the
entire, normal course of its own evolution into and then
as a capitalist country. But in fact the Communist revolutions have occurred and succeeded, thus far invariably,
in decidedly backward or underdeveloped, never more than
incipiently modern-capitalist, countries. And I think we
shall find in this fact, and in the reasons for it, the main

explanation both of the morally worst features and of the widespread, strong appeal and great power of modern Communism.

That the actual, modern development in this respect has been so contrary to what Marx expected simply brings to light, I think, one of his serious mistakes or errors. He was mistaken in his belief that the mass poverty, misery, and radical discontent that were widely prevalent in his time in the Western world, in an early stage of its development of or into the age and system of industrial capitalism or capitalist industrialism, would grow worse and worse in the further course of that development; that the system would evolve in such a way as to make it work ever less well for the welfare of labor and of most of the people, and become intolerable and ripe for destruction and replacement by socialism, only in its old age. In actual fact, the worst conditions and discontents and largest degrees of readiness for revolutionary change of that kind have existed in every country in that transitional phase of its own development in which it was just beginning to emerge out of long ages of stagnant, preindustrial and largely precapitalist feudalism, or something like that, into the first, as yet more disturbing or upsetting than plainly beneficial stages of the growth of progressive, industrial capitalism. Wherever the latter has had a fair chance to go on developing and maturing under at all favorable conditions, it has in time grown not worse but better, worked increasingly well for the welfare of the people of all classes, helped to bring about intellectual, cultural, moral, and institutional as well as economic progress, undergone and in time accepted many detailed reforms, and won increasingly general and full acceptance and stability or viability. But while the Western world since Marx's time has thus moved not into but away from the "revolutionary situation" that was almost there in his day, the most extreme and fanatical of his latter-day disciples, the modern Communists, have been able to win their triumphs in Russia, China, and so on, because in those countries the delayed beginnings of industrialization under capitalist auspices, along with other circumstances, there brought fully into being revolutionary situations of the kind which the Marxists, in spite of Marx's opinion to the contrary, were best able to exploit.

Let me just briefly mention the generally known conditions that existed in those now Communist-ruled countries just before their Communist revolutions occurred. Their peoples had lived for ages under really oppressive social class hierarchies and at once cruel and feeble governments by and for their upper classes. Real, intense mass poverty and misery were there and stagnant, unprogressive economies and cultures. And the great and growing disparities between those countries and the more advanced and progressive Western, liberal capitalist countries, caused the small but potent groups of Western-educated, native intellectuals in the backward areas to feel intensely, patriotically ashamed of the conditions of their countries and fervently ambitious to bring about swift, radical changes. There appeared to be virtually no prospects or possibilities of achieving peaceful, gradual reforms, and in any case there was no patience for that course. Also, despite or along with the influence of Western education and ideas there was also the influence of the old, native, spiritual cultures which tended to produce the kind of naive, visionary mentality that is most susceptible to the appeal of Marxism in its own most visionary, fervent, grandiose, and radical form and aspect. Moreover, the Communist movements in these countries have promised from the outset and, in degrees that we must not underestimate, have been achieving rapid industrialization and modernization of the entire national economies and societies and something like all-around progress although with fatal omissions in the field of ethical or moral progress. No doubt it has seemed and seems to very many of the bright aspiring, patriotic people in those countries—although I am sure that in this judgment they are tragically mistaken— that all of the tyranny or despotism, violence, coercion, cruelty, and so on, involved in the process of achieving forced and rapid "progress" in this way, amount only to a small and necessary price to pay for it and all the benefits they are sure it will bring to their countries and their peoples in future generations.

I have still to explain, however, the feature of the development of the ideas and attitudes of the modern Communists, from and beyond those of Marx, which seems to me to underlie or constitute the deeply, morally evil aspect of Communism and present the main moral issue in our conflict with it. Let me refer back to what I said earlier about the relative emphasis in the thought of Marx on evolutionary social progress and on revolutions. By and large, as I have pointed out, since Marx's time, most non-Communist, Western socialists including the still nominally Marxist social democrats have gradually shifted all of their emphasis to exclusive faith in and work for evolutionary progress or entirely away from the revolutionary frame of mind. The modern Communists, on the contrary—thanks in part I think to the Russian origin and mainly Oriental career of Communism thus far—have put their main emphasis, much more strongly than Marx did, on the revolutionary side of Marxism; and have greatly developed its cold theory and practice of the most effective, never morally inhibited, revolutionary strategy and tactics. Now of course we heirs and adherents of the general tradition of Western liberalism cannot consistently condemn or oppose on moral grounds all revolutions in all circumstances. When masses of men are really driven in desperation, by really extreme and not otherwise remediable oppression and injustice and horrible conditions, into really inevitable, spontaneous, impassioned, revolutionary or warlike action for radical change and improvement and led to do the things or use the methods that are necessary for victory in and belong to wars and revolutions, one cannot blame them and must sympathize with them and may well be justified in praising them; and the long-run sum of the results may well include more good than evil, though I think the moral costs of violent revolutions are always serious and the moral gains are often dubious and in general revolutions are not things to be indiscriminately or lightly in favor of. But spontaneous, necessary revolution, really produced simply by unendurable evils and human-natural responses to them, is one thing, and cold, intellectual self-schooling in a wholly Machiavellian or amoral theory of how to anticipate, induce, conduct, control, and exploit revolutions wherever and whenever they become possible is something else. And this is what the modern Communists practice in the most thoroughgoing way, and what makes them the pestilence they are in the world today. The appealing, utopian idealism which is also included in their outlook—the bright vision of progress to the impossible heaven-on-earth of a perfect, spontaneous cooperation of all mankind for the common welfare of all —is more than nullified in practical effect, even where it is sincere, by being combined with their utterly hard-boiled philosophy and systematic use of every kind of violence, deception, treachery, and brutal compulsion as means, supposedly, of working toward that alluring end. As many before me have pointed out, extensive, deliberate, systematic use of evil means in the effort to attain good ends invariably makes the end-results actually attained not good but evil.

There is still much more to be said, however—indeed much more of course than I will have time to say here— about the Communist philosophy and actual system and their contrasts with our Western liberal philosophy and system and the elements and grounds of our proper, intelligent faith in the moral and general superiority and eventual triumph of the things we stand for. One part of the Communist philosophy that plays so important a part in their propaganda and our struggle with them that I must say a few, necessarily inadequate words about it is the theory, developed by Lenin and others, of what they call monopoly capitalism and capitalist imperialism. I have already explained what I think is the real reason why all the Communist revolutions have occurred, thus far, not in the advanced or fully developed capitalist countries, as Marx prophesied, but in Russia first and then in other, still more backward, underdeveloped countries on the outer fringes of the capitalist world and still, before their revolutions, in the first or early stages of their own evolutions into capitalist countries. But the Communist theory of capitalist imperialism was developed and used by Lenin to explain all this in a different way, for the case of Russia, and has since become the great intellectual tool and weapon of the Communists for identifying their ambitions with the aspirations of all the underdeveloped countries and exploiting the grievances of the latter against the Western, capitalist world. According to Lenin, by or before 1917, the evolving, economic systems of the larger, Western, advanced capitalist countries had become systems of monopoly capitalism, that is, national economies dominated by small numbers of gigantic firms, trusts, cartels, or unified or centralized, industrial and financial empires, enjoying and exploiting monopoly powers in their national and world markets and able to control the domestic and foreign policies of their national governments. And this growth of monopolies, or decline of competition within the mature national capitalisms, had created dilemmas for the great capitalists themselves that they could resolve or alleviate only by pressuring their governments into imperialistic, aggressive foreign policies or adventures to gain control of the backward, underdeveloped parts of the world and the economic resources, labor, and potential markets in them for the benefit of the great capitalists at home. By using their monopoly powers in their domestic product-markets and labor-markets to obtain high prices and pay low wages, the big business groups increased the difficulty, always severe in capitalism according to Marx, of finding adequate, profitable outlets or markets for their full, potential outputs and investment-outlets for their growing masses of accumulating capital. High prices and low wages in the home economies would lead to underconsumption or overproduction there and general depression unless the big profits gained as long as that was avoided were invested not in expanding plant-capacity and production for the home market, but in exporting goods and capital to exclusively controlled, foreign, undeveloped areas. With the aid of this theory, Lenin contended that the entire world, regardless of the stages of development of individual countries, was all falling under domination and exploitation by the big capitalists in the big, advanced capitalist, Western countries or great powers. So the world-revolution didn't have to begin within the advanced countries, as Marx had thought it would; the world-economy was becoming unified and was threatened with control or enslavement throughout by the capitalist groups in the big Western countries, and the process of "liberating" the world from their control could and should begin in the part of the world where their power was newest and as yet weakest. Czarist Russia, according to Lenin, was already one of the great powers and a half-developed, capitalist country but the weakest link in the chain of the imperialist powers, and it was intelligent strategy for the revolution to break the chain by breaking, first, its weakest link. In the subsequent decades it has been easy, of course, for the Communists to make this theory of the necessarily imperialistic nature and policies of all the Western, advanced capitalist countries and the menace to all underdeveloped countries represented by them, a very potent propaganda weapon for use in all the less developed countries and against the Western world.

I wish I had time here to properly dissect this theory of "imperialism," to separate the few grains of truth from the mass of falsehood and nonsense in it, and to suggest a correct view of the problems involved, but I cannot do all that in the time available. Let me say only the following things about the subject. "Imperialism" in the proper sense of the word—the tendencies of strong or powerful nations and states to become aggressive and expansive and extend their power over or control and subjugate initially foreign territories and peoples—is as old as human history and was at its worst in ages long before the development anywhere of modern capitalism or the modern business economy; and has been declining within the capitalist world and era, slowly, ever since the liberal ideals of the proper freedoms of all men and nations became important in our Western culture, in and after the eighteenth century Enlightenment, and began to affect prevailing, Western attitudes and actual policies. For the main sources or causes of imperialism do not lie in the economic needs or necessities and political

powers of big business concerns and groups. The roles they
sometimes play or appear to play are generally incidental
and secondary and arise less from their inabilities to avoid
in any other way the alleged dilemma described in the
Communist theory than from circumstances and requirements incidental to their beneficial contributions to the
development of underdeveloped countries and from involve-
ments with the more or less necessary, strategic, national
defense policies of their countries, and sometimes partly
from unnecessary, business and patriotic megalomania and
unwise and illiberal attitudes toward native populations,
societies, and problems. The main cause of the persistence
of imperialism in the modern world is the anarchic and
chaotic nature of the world of sovereign national states
under no international government or effective body of
international law, the insecurity of all states and their mutual fears and animosities, and the imperative need of each
great power for enough control of the strategically important but internally weak or weakly governed and defended
parts of the world to prevent their being controlled and
used against it by its likely enemies. The foreign policies
that can be called imperialistic generally originate mainly
not in the economic needs or ambitions of business groups,
but in the anxieties of statesmen, responsible for the security
of their countries in the event of war, to extend and maintain the power and influence of their countries in the vital
regions from that point of view. The business groups which
go along or get involved may profit by and support these
policies for business reasons, but they are seldom the prime

movers. The Communist myth that imperialism is rooted or inherent, and uniquely so, in the nature of fully developed capitalism, and the Communist theory's confusion of brutal and injurious, domineering imperialism in the proper sense of the word, with all participation by Western business men and investors in the economic development of underdeveloped countries, are both potent, false, and devilish parts of the creed or mythology with which we are contending.

But now I must conclude this lecture with a few words about what seems to me our own main, general problem, in our American and Western, liberal world, of sufficiently realizing or living up to our own best, liberal ideals in conducting both all domestic and all foreign affairs to make the superiority, for human welfare in every sense, of our actual, social system and civilization, over that which is being developed in the Communist world, evident and convincing to the world in general. In the necessary effort to do this we face many difficulties because there are always, in this imperfect world of imperfect human beings and societies, shocking gaps between all high or worthy ideals and the average, actual practices even of those who are most sincerely devoted to them. The gap between the ideals of Western liberalism at its best and the actual behavior-patterns of our Western nations and their citizens individually and as groups and their governments, in all internal and foreign dealings, is as nothing when compared with the gap between the vague but attractive, promised, future utopia and the currently existing, actual system, of Communism. But the Communists have in a way a psychological

advantage over us in appealing to the naive minds of mul-
titudes of simple people, because the Communists admit that
their current practices are not on the ideal plane of the
utopia or perfected, socialist world toward which they pro-
fess to be leading mankind, and excuse their current practices as necessary, temporary expedients in the great work
of building that far better, future world. And the naive
millions everywhere have great capacities for believing both
that a utopian or perfect world must be attainable if those
who know the way to it lead the way and are followed, and
that even the worst evils and hardships may be well worth
enduring in the present and even throughout one's own
lifetime, if they are but the necessary price of enabling one's
children to enter utopia or the promised land. Our Western
liberalism on the other hand, though belief in the possibility
of progress to a better future has been a part of it, has generally demanded of its adherents that they live up now and
all the time to its best ideals and has made their failures to
do so, fully, appear to put their ideals and professions into
the category of hypocritical pretensions or illusions. We
face a manifold task of reducing the not totally removable
difficulties of our situation, in all possible ways, to safe,
minimal dimensions. We need to clarify and improve the
generally accepted formulation of our ideals—our liberal
philosophy—to make it all at once clear, consistent, morally
valid and appealing to the conscience of mankind, and
realistic in the sense of realizable, approximately or nearly
enough, under existing and prospective, real conditions, and
increasingly, progressively, as we make progress both in

controlling and suitably modifying those conditions and in improving our habitual practices toward fuller conformity with our best ideals. At the same time we must be humble enough to acknowledge the faults of our actual, imperfect societies and practices and present not them as they are but our ideals to the world as the things we stand and strive and fight for, while also working to realize our ideals more fully in practice, and convince the world of our sincerity. One part of our difficulty is that our traditional philosophy, the classical Western liberalism, has become altered in diverse quarters within our own world in diverse ways, and we have a confusion of creeds and moral visions instead of general agreement on a single sound one, and too much disillusioned cynicism and lack of any firm and strong idealism is widespread among us. There is need, I think, for a new revival, with appropriate revisions in view of modern realities and modern knowledge, of the liberal idealism which inspired the best Western intellectual and political leaders of the late eighteenth and the nineteenth century, including the founding fathers of this country. And I shall try, in my next and final lecture in this series, to suggest the shape or some of the elements of the modern liberal vision or philosophy that I think we need.

Chapter IV ~ REVISING OUR LIBERAL
PHILOSOPHY IN OUR CHANGING WORLD

As compared with my previous lectures, this final one has a less direct or immediate reference to our struggle with the Communist world, or is more exclusively directed inward, so to speak, in reflection upon our own American and Western world or civilization, and traditions of liberal-democratic and economic-liberal thought and practice and present-day, internal problems. But I think the internal task, which would lie before us in any case, of improving the conduct of our own affairs is by no means unrelated to the other, current task, which tends to preoccupy us, of defending our civilization in its conflict with the Communist world and movement, and if possible insuring the eventual triumph of the ideals we stand for in the world at large. In the last analysis, our liberal or free civilization can overcome the Communist challenge only by maintaining and improving its own health, vitality, viability, and ability to cope with its own problems—both old, continuing, and new, modern problems—and the intrinsic attractiveness of its creed and practices to the reason, aspirations, and conscience of mankind. The strength or potency of the Communist challenge is directly related to the weaknesses within our own civilization or social, political, and economic systems and effective culture and morality. Communist feeling and thought, insofar as they have a real basis, are based on discernment and exaggeration of some evils, real to some extent, in the capitalistic or *bourgeois* civilization, and the effort to develop a radically different, alternative system alleged to be without those or any evils. The clear facts that the Communist criticism grossly misrepresents our actual system and exaggerates its evils and that the Communist alternative is really a mass of far worse evils do not alter the fact that the real imperfections in our system of beliefs and practices underlie or contribute to the appeal of Communism to a large part of mankind, and thus to its power. Informing the world of the facts as they are can, I think, do much to refute and overcome the Communist challenge, but the defense of our civilization requires also that we make, as we need to make anyway, all the progress that we can in improving it and thus making it still more defensible.

Now I think our modern difficulties, in making headway in this general task, are much increased by, on the one hand, the complexity of our liberal, democratic, and capitalistic system and civilization, or the endlessness of the mass and variety of its detailed features and detailed problems and, on the other hand, the long growing tendency of all or most modern thought to become exclusively immersed in or preoccupied with empirical and practical details of diverse kinds and lose the all-inclusive vision of the whole and the grasp of fundamental, general principles without which we lose our way and become victims of growing and multiplying, intellectual and moral confusions. Wisdom can be developed only by the kind of continuing, collaborative, empirical *and rational* inquiry and reflection that makes full use not only of all the resources of experience and empirical research, but also of all of the capacity of human reason, or rational or at once imaginative and logical reflection, to grasp or envisage the unity and order of the universe of data, and the logical system of general principles exemplified in all of it. In past ages, from antiquity down through medieval into modern times, the chief, prevailing weakness of most Western thought was overconfidence in the power of pure reason and the adequacy of abstract, general principles and lack of sufficient development and use of accurate, detailed, empirical knowledge. That error or mistaken tendency first began to be overcome in and by the intellectual revolution of the seventeenth century, in philosophy and the sciences, which ended the reign of the antique, one-sided, absolute rationalism and substituted for it the valid epistemology and methodology of rational empiricism—a mode of thought equally attentive to the insights of reason and the facts of experience. The immediate fruit of that revolution in our field of interest was the eighteenth century Enlightenment, which carried the new way of seeking wisdom or understanding over from and beyond the natural sciences into the social and moral sciences and laid the intellectual and moral foundations of our modern, Western civilization by creating the over-all social and moral philosophy which on the whole it has ever since been trying and tending to develop and realize or carry out in practice—the classical liberalism.

This was and is, in aim at least, a philosophy grounded in or appealing to the immediate experiences of all men as individuals, of their desires and situations, *and* their power to achieve a common, reasoned understanding of the conditions or requirements of the fullest possible, continuing, all-around satisfaction or fulfillment of the needs of all in the changing, real, empirical world. The new emphasis upon experience was as yet fortunately still combined with a strong, continuing emphasis upon the use or exercise of reason to envision and analyze or elaborate the system of general principles which must be made effective in and through the institutions and operating processes of liberal democracy, the liberal system of law or legal justice, and the liberal economy if the true, particular, and common interests of all are indeed to be well served. So it is not accidental or inappropriate that the great age of the liberal Enlightenment, which gave us the basic design of our civilization, has also gone down in history as the Age of Reason.

The then new or novel side, however, of the mode of thought of that epoch was not its rationalism or faith in reason but its empiricism or desire to ground its principles in directly experienced facts and values. In the subsequent development of Western culture there has been a growing, unfortunate, and mistaken tendency to swing too far toward the opposite extreme from that of the antique, absolute rationalism, that is, toward an absolute kind of empiricism and pragmatism, concerned only with efforts to add to and use detailed, empirical knowledge in special fields, and solve particular, detailed, practical problems one at a time and failing to retain and go on developing anything like an adequate, rational, theoretical, or philosophical vision of the liberal design of our civilization and the general principles that must be generally understood and observed if it is to be realized. Moreover, this ultramodern decline of confidence in the power of reason to apprehend the true, general principles of the social and moral order has been going on especially with regard to those normative, ethical principles which must make up the essence of a rational liberalism. In the natural sciences, in which no questions arise concerning what the universe of nature ought to be—since man is not the designer and builder but only a user of that universe—and the search is only for knowledge and understanding of its actual structure and processes, the on-going progress of rational, theoretical research has not faltered as compared with that of experimental and observational or all empirical research nor fallen behind the latter nor into any undue or improper subordination to it. And in the social sciences insofar as they also are or can be simply positive sciences, seeking knowledge and understanding of the actual structures and functionings of existing, actual, human societies, theoretical research has in general held its own fairly well and is beginning to get effectively interrelated with the modern, advancing techniques and developments of social-scientific, empirical research. But human societies, as human creations, are not only subject to positive or scientific laws or principles, the study of which can show us how they will function and develop if and as long as they are constituted in certain ways; they also are subject to, that is, need to be developed in accordance with, normative, ethical or moral laws or principles which their human members and creators must discover and obey in order to so constitute them that they will function and develop in line with the real requirements of the real, true welfare of mankind. In all the past ages, including that of the liberal Enlightenment, in which a full and consistent recognition of this truth prevailed, the studies that we now call the social sciences or their forerunners in those times were always called the moral sciences and conceived not as entirely or solely positive sciences of or about existing actual societies, but as also normative inquiries, or branches of ethical or moral philosophy, endeavoring to ascertain and formulate the truly obligatory, moral principles by which men must be guided in forming and operating good societies as conducive as possible to good lives for all their members. But there has been going on of late and for a long time a spreading decline of real belief in the reality and cognizability of any such rational, moral principles or the possibility of any rational, ethical wisdom, applicable as such in the conduct of all private and public affairs. And the result has been that we have tended increasingly to try to conduct our affairs with the aid only of diverse and discordant, unreasoned sentiments or feelings on all moral questions, together with our growing and improving knowledge of all kinds of current, actual situations, and the likely consequences of alternative courses of action, and the courses needed to bring about the results desired by those whose feelings or sentiments prevail in the making of particular decisions.

Now the moral use of reason, which has thus been tending to become a lost art within our culture, is indeed a very difficult art—even more difficult to explain than to practice —and I cannot take time here to say more than a few words about its nature. The seeker of reasoned, moral wisdom, or knowledge of the principles which ought to guide us in the conduct of all public affairs, needs the fullest, universal width or breadth of outlook on the lives, affairs, and interests not of some but of all human beings and on all departments of their lives. What is good or right, period, means not what is good for this or that interest-pressure-group, class, or nation but what is good for all, together; and it means not what is good economically, or for prosperity, or good from any other one limited or special standpoint but what is good for the all-around and well-balanced, material and spiritual welfare of all men. Thus the moral philosopher needs, ideally, to be conversant with all sciences and arts, all human knowledge, and the complete, real worlds and lives of all men and societies; and to have in his heart and imagination, steadily, universal and impartial or well-balanced sympathies with all the aspirations of all human beings. Of course, this ideal is unattainable; to realize it, literally, would be to be omniscient, and that is why all human moral judgments are deficient and diverse, and why we have in our religion the idea of the all-knowing and all-loving God, on the revelation of whose divine wisdom and will we are dependent. And yet in the Christian tradition we think, too, that we can and should have something of that all-knowing and all-loving spirit in ourselves; the word "conscience"—con plus science—literally means, knowing all things together. Among our intellectual disciplines, philosophy in the ancient sense, the love or pursuit of wisdom, is the effort to approach, though it cannot reach, this all-inclusive, over-all, synoptic, general comprehension of all existence and all values. The best attainable, rational ethics necessarily is, I think, the crown or culmination of philosophy in that sense, and the modern, relative decline of faith in the possibility of a rational ethics is largely a result of the decline of the cultivation and prestige of philosophy in the ancient sense, in our age of advancing, multiplying, and ever-narrowing specializations. All our special sciences and arts of course have their important values, but the trend to increasing fragmentation and chaos in our culture needs to be counteracted by combining with the progress of ever more detailed analysis in every special field, an equal progress of the effort to achieve a new, modern, intellectual synthesis of the most general principles of all of them into the principles of a modern, all-embracing philosophy and code of ethics.

Now the last or most recent period in the history of Western intellectual life and culture that did achieve and have such a synthesis of all then existing knowledge was the eighteenth century Enlightenment, and the fruit of its synthesis was the classical, liberal philosophy and ethics. And I think our modern task is really that of further modernizing, or revising in adjustment to all the newer elements of modern life and knowledge, the still essentially true and wise principles of the classical liberalism. The wisdom of those principles, moreover, resides very largely in the way in which they recognize and take into account, and find or contrive the best way around, the insurmountable difficulty or impossibility of real attainment by any one person or group in authority of anything like full or adequate wisdom about the detailed, special situations, natures, needs, and true interests of all the different members of society. The liberal solution of this fundamental problem, arising from the inevitable limitations of all human wisdoms, is to aim only at devising and developing a system of institutions impartially protecting the equal liberties of all men to achieve and use the knowledge of their own situations and true interests which they can achieve, and at the same time enabling and helping them continually to adjust their relations with each other into a pattern such that everyone's best way of serving his own interests will lie in the courses of action which in fact also best serve the interests of others, and the common interest of them all.

One essential part of the liberal scheme of institutions is the liberal legal order, or system of law or legal justice, which should impartially protect or enforce the equal and reciprocal rights and duties among all and prevent, with the minimal or most humane, sufficient, deterrent penalties, all commissions by anyone of any actions yielding private gains to him or serving or advancing his special interests in ways involving injustices or injuries to others or the common welfare. Then a second, essential part of the liberal scheme of institutions is the economic system of free, private enterprises and open, free, or competitive markets, which, if it operates within the framework of the liberal system of legal justice, can enable all to reward each other for desired services and best serve their own interests by best serving, or helping to satisfy, each other's needs and wants. With the legal order closing to all alike all doors to private gains through injuries to others, the liberal economy can open to all alike all doors to private gains through services to others, and the two together can thus largely create an effective harmony of or among the interests of all.

Then also, since public institutions must be created and, in a changing world, continually developed and modified in details, through a political and governmental process, a third, essential part of the liberal system is its political and governmental system, liberal democracy; which again endeavors to balance and combine the interests or desires and the portions or areas of knowledge and wisdom and the views of all; or endeavors to enable all to contribute, through public discussion and mutual persuasion or compromise, to the shaping of governmental decisions and actions, which may thus be made as just to all as possible. There is an important distinction, however, between liberal democracy and simple or absolute democracy; both in their fullest developments involve universal suffrage and majority rule, but while absolute democracy would mean an absolute or unlimited right or power of the popular majority to do whatever it may want to do, liberal democracy means majority rule limited by impartial, constitutional protections of the essential liberties and rights of all minorities and all individuals. Absolute democracy can be as illiberal, despotic, authoritarian, or totalitarian as any system; only liberal democracy can be a part of, or consistent with, the liberal social and moral order.

Let me also in passing emphasize another distinction, a distinction between two things which I may call ethical democracy and mechanical democracy. By ethical democracy I mean the prevalence in a society of a general spirit or set of attitudes tending toward humane concern on the parts of all for the liberties, rights, and welfare of all, hence leading those in authority to work sincerely for the welfare of all the people, and leading the people to welcome all measures that are both conducive to their welfares and consistent with the just rights and the welfare of all and to be critical of and resistant to all despotic measures which are in flagrant violation of those standards. Mechanical democracy, on the other hand, is any system of specific, institutional or constitutional and political mechanisms, designed to insure or enforce, as well as any mechanisms can do this, responsibility and responsiveness of the governors to the governed and equal opportunities for all of the governed to make their desires and knowledge and views count in the public process of discussion and decision-making. Most Americans today are far too prone to embrace the absurd belief that all societies or countries in the world should immediately adopt, and could immediately, effectively achieve and operate, exactly the kind of democratic, governmental, and political system in the mechanical sense that we have in this country. Evolutions toward eventual, real achievement and effective use of liberal-democratic, political systems or mechanisms, adapted to the diverse, particular characters and needs of particular countries, are I think indeed desirable in all cases, for the spirit of ethical democracy can become fully developed, prevalent, and effective only with the instrumental aid of such mechanisms. But the mechanisms without the spirit are worse than useless; and on the other hand there often can be much development of or toward the spirit and its general prevalence, and much production by it alone of many of the benefits of real democracy, even in the absence of anything like a democratic, political mechanism. And until this prior, fundamental development of the spirit pervading a society has advanced to a certain point, and numerous other conditions have been fulfilled, such a mechanism cannot be introduced and used and made to do more good than harm.

Liberal democracy—meaning now both the spirit and the mechanism together, or the best approximation to both and to each at its best that we have achieved, say, in this country —liberal democracy is by no means the least difficult part of the liberal system to achieve, maintain, and operate well and is perennially confronted with many serious problems. Here I can only touch upon a few of them and may in this passage say only obvious things. We have never yet, with all our efforts, succeeded in educating the entire mass of all our citizens well enough to qualify them properly for participation in the democratic process. Nor have we adequately retained or continued from predemocratic times, with the needed adjustments into harmony with our democracy, the kind of leadership of our society and government by the members of that minority of the able, wise, and good that must exist in every decent, great society and needs to play its role in even the most democratic society. Our American democracy has tended too largely to become the victim of the following vicious circle. First, the abundance and variety of opportunities in our society for successful, constructive, and interesting, purely private careers and lives has drawn too many of our ablest and best potential leaders away from entry into public life, into purely private pursuits. Thus too many of our politicians and public men have been mediocrities and have tended in too many cases to make their political careers roads to private wealth, power, and enjoyment, achieved by serving their particular groups of constituents and supporters according to not their real needs but their ignorant wants and in ways often inconsistent with the equal rights and the common welfare of all Americans. Then next, we have as a nation tended to adopt a far too cynical view of the supposed, inevitable nature of all politics and politicians and refused to reward political and public service with the kind of respect, prestige, and honor that alone could make it attractive to our best qualified, potential leaders. All this, however, is only one phase of the problem of securing the best democratic political leadership. Still another source of our difficulties in this matter lies I think in the growing gulf, in our increasingly complex intellectual and practical culture, between the true intellectuals or unusually able and well-educated minds and the mass of the people; and in two results of that gulf—the too frequent tendency of intellectuals to overestimate their own shares of wisdom and adopt conceited, arrogant, superior attitudes, and the natural, retaliatory tendency of the common people and the less intellectually brilliant and well-educated men of action or affairs to develop an anti-intellectual attitude of suspicion and hostility toward all "egg-heads," and refuse to accept or follow them as leaders. The democratic equality of all men in its true meaning, of course, does not mean that all men are equal in ability, in wisdom, or in virtue; or that the inferior majority should be jealous or resentful of the superior degrees of power and influence which should be exerted by superior men, or unwilling to respect and defer to their wiser judgments. But it does mean that all men are equally entitled to their country's equal concern for their rights and best potential developments and welfares, and that even the ablest and wisest should always have and show their proper shares of humility, or awareness of the limitations of their shares of wisdom, and respect for the shares of experience and common sense of all ordinary men as needed supplements and correctives to their own advanced and specialized attainments.

There remains one further aspect of this matter of the kind of leadership needed within a democracy, insofar as that involves leadership-roles for intellectuals, about which I must say a word. The modern growth of specialization among intellectuals—of multiplying and narrowing, scientific and applied-scientific or technical specialties, and the concomitant decline of philosophy and the number of very broadly educated, informed, and thoughtful men—has been bringing about a situation in which most of the intellectuals who play any part in the work of democratic governments, play their parts simply as employed experts in their various technical specialties, who conduct inquiries and make recommendations on particular problems in particular departments. This of course is necessary and excellent as far as it goes, but it is not the leadership I have been discussing. It is only a matter of helping the real, final makers of the important decisions on public policies of all kinds to ascertain the most effective methods, means and routes toward the end-results which are desired by the policy-makers and those whose wishes they must heed and serve, the most numerous or most influential politicians and voters. What we need and too largely lack is intellectual or wise leadership at this other point—a leadership able to lead the politicians and voters toward desires or value-judgments enlightened by adequate, general or broad understanding of all the possible, alternative policy-goals and ways of attaining them and of all the likely costs and consequences of alternative choices for the welfares of all who will be affected by them. In other words, we need in the highest positions in our governments more statesmen who can bring to their tasks not only good "briefings" by all kinds of experts or technicians, but ample stores of very broadly informed and reflective, social- and moral-philosophic wisdom of their own. While we want our democracies to be and remain democracies, not societies ruled by Platonic philosopher-kings, they should be led by philosopher-states-men, gifted in the art of rational persuasion of the people, and responsive not to the people's ignorant or misguided demands, but to those they would make if they were more enlightened.

But now let me turn from this discussion of some of the problems of political democracy, to one of the central, general problems of the liberal, institutional system as a whole —the problem of the proper or best division of labor, or of functions and spheres of free operation, between the liberal-democratic state and government, or political and governmental system, on the one hand, and the liberal economy or economic system of private enterprises, households, and markets, on the other hand. To what extent and in what respects and ways should the structure, working, and development of the economy be controlled by governmental actions, determined through the democratic, political process? What parts of all that goes on within the economy, or the sphere of men's economic activities and relations, should be directly controlled, and how, by the government and what and how much should be "let alone" by it and determined by free, private choices or decisions and the free play of competitive pressures and market forces or the so-called laws of supply and demand? Are there any, today still valid, general principles of liberal thought to guide us to the correct answers to more specific questions in this field? I think it is in the field of this general problem, that is, in the politico-economic department of liberal thought, that some of the worst, now very widespread, intellectual and moral confusions have arisen in modern thought and public opinion in all Western countries, in or from the recent evolutions of their real economic, social, and political systems, practices, and conditions, and thought about the resulting problems. The old or classical, economic liberalism stood for a simple, sharp separation of the political and economic spheres, or a very strict limitation of the powers or rights of governments to interfere in or with or act upon the economic system, and great reliance upon the automatic, self-adjusting and self-regulating processes of the economy itself to maintain its own good order and appropriate, socially beneficial functioning and development. But today in marked contrast with that outlook and program, the kind of outlook and program that is now more commonly in political discourse called liberal, especially in this country, argues for a great expansion of the sphere of governmental efforts to control or influence the economy and its working and development and change the effective distribution of wealth and income in favor of wage-earners, farmers, and low-income groups, and control and abolish or at least greatly moderate the cycle of alternating general business booms and depressions, or stabilize the economy at or near the so-called full employment level or volume of activity.

In my own opinion, the wise and right course for governmental policy relating to the economy would lie somewhere between these extremes of full or strict *laissez faire* and the semi-socialistic, so-called liberalism of today. But exactly where in that range it should lie and what its guiding principles should be is by no means easy to say or know, and I will not be able here to get beyond a few rather vague and not very useful generalities about this matter. I think there is no doubt that a good many, substantial changes away from adherence to the pure, strict precepts of the old economic liberalism have been made necessary or desirable by the growths of newer, modern conditions and problems and by recent advances of modern knowledge. But the kind of revision of or departure from the old economic liberalism that is represented by our modern liberals, now commonly so-called, seems to me to be not a coherent, rational, or sound one, but a rather chaotic mass of *ad hoc* expedients and irrational, emotional or sentimental views of the ends to be aimed at or values to be realized; and this I think is potentially at least as dangerous to the freedoms for all and justice among all and the order and progress that we need in our economy and society, as any excessive reaction toward the old, strict *laissez faire* regime would be. What we need and lack is a real, rational revision and new, modern development of the old, politico-economic, liberal phi-losophy—a modern, clear and consistent and valid system of both economic and ethical, fundamental, general princi-ples, inspired by the old and authentic liberal, libertarian spirit but applying that with a full, realistic grasp of all the relevant, present-day conditions and problems and with full use of all relevant, available, modern knowledge. I have not worked this out and could not present it tonight if I had, but I want in the remaining time to say a few more things that I think point in the right direction. But first, I want to indicate a rarely mentioned part of what seems to me the valid basis of the view that we should maintain, though not exactly as prescribed by the old *laissez faire* gospel, a fairly clear and careful separation of the political and economic spheres, or limitation of the role or functions of the democratic state and government and political process, in relation to the operation and development of what should remain our liberal economy.

The economic part of life, or men's economic choices or decisions and activities, can and should be directed, governed, or guided to a large extent by a degree and kind or rationality which cannot play the same role in the democratic, political process or in the making of governmental decisions controlled by it for reasons inherent in the inevitable and appropriate nature of that process. The managers of business enterprises and of households, if they have adequate freedom, opportunity, and knowledge, can arrive at and carry out reasonably rational decisions, fitting into and making up a consistent, continuing practice of true, rational "economy," or the best use of all their available resources of all kinds to attain most fully, together, all the ends, or satisfy, in a good balance, all the wants, which make competing demands on those resources. Rational economy or economic rationality in this sense extends a little way beyond the sphere, and hence inevitably falls, in its character, a little way below the standards, of the kind of really exact and rigorous rationality which is at home in the pure and applied physical sciences. For the comparative estimating, weighing, or balancing against one another, of not only diverse physical and monetary quantities but also diverse human desires and values, which is involved in the practice or pursuit of rational economy, involves the effort to combine with as much as possible of applied-scientific rationality an element of that other and by scientific standards necessarily inferior or more dubious kind of rationality to which I referred earlier in referring to the ethical or moral use of reason. Moreover, of course, in passing from the idea of rational, detached thinking about problems to that of rational conduct or behavior, we are bound to encounter fresh difficulties; and much weight must be granted to the views of those modern psychologists, anthropologists, and sociologists who hold that little or no human behavior is or can be fully rational—that most of it is more influenced by irrational or at least nonrational, emotional-and-mental energies and processes than by rational comparisons of the probable costs and benefits connected with the alternative, possible courses of behavior. Too many economists have exaggerated the possibility of making all economic theory perfectly rational or scientific throughout, and too many, in their assumptions about the prevailing character of human, economic behavior in the liberal economy, have still more seriously exaggerated the probable extent to which it is or can be rational, even under the best conditions. Nevertheless, even when all that has been said and allowed for, it remains true I think that the field of economic life is one in which, as compared with most other departments of life, a somewhat especially, relatively high degree of or near approach to rationality is possible; and the nearest possible approach to it is certainly desirable. As I have said, intelligent managers of firms and households, the units making up the economy, if they have the necessary freedoms, opportunities, and knowledge, can generally make reasonably rational decisions on the ways of using their resources to attain their ends that can be expected at least roughly or nearly to maximize the gains or benefits or satisfactions attained, relative to the costs necessarily incurred. And through an appropriate set or system of market and price mechanisms, the decisions made in all the different firms and households, or economic units, which are rational from the standpoints of their private interests, can be reciprocally adjusted and related in such a way that the resulting pattern of the uses made of the economy's resources and productive efforts to produce and distribute satisfactions of the wants of the people will be rational from the standpoint of the general welfare of the entire community. Let it be acknowledged that the best really possible, practical realization of this ideal vision is bound to be imperfect not only because economic behavior is at best imperfectly rational, but also because, under real conditions, the adjustments achieved through actual market and price mechanisms are bound to be at best imperfect. Still I think it is true that a reasonably, approximately liberal economy, in which most economic decisions are freely made by the persons or groups or units nearest to and most familiar with the immediately relevant facts and values, and in which the connections and adjustments among all those decisions are worked out through impersonal, market processes of roughly the liberal or

free and competitive kind—such an economy can operate
more rationally or effectively in the service of the general
welfare than can an economy in which too many of the
more important decisions are made or controlled by distant,
central, governmental authorities who are in turn controlled, as they should be, by the democratic, political process. For it belongs to the nature of political life and behavior and the democratic process to be less rational, in
the sense or by the standards here in question, than free,
private, economic behavior can be and tends to be. And it
follows that the field of matters over which the democratic, political process should have control does not include much in the field of direct economic decision-making.

Let me a little more fully explain this point about the
only half-rational and half-emotional nature of political
life and thought and the democratic process, and the class
of social or public problems they are best adapted for deal-
ing with. What I am trying to express here is not at all an
adverse criticism of the normal operation of political
democracy in its proper sphere, but only an objective
characterization of it and of that sphere in comparison or
contrast with the simpler and in a simple sense more largely
rational, potential, and appropriate nature of economic life
and the economic sphere. The main or principal proper
function of the democratic political process is to shape and
reshape, in adaptation to the changing circumstances, needs,
and desires of the people and all groups among them, all
the general laws which together make up the order or system of legal justice—which in the relevant aspects, in rela-

tion to the economy, is the framework of legal limits around all areas of free, private, economic choices and activities, a framework that should impartially protect the just rights of all, or prevent any person or group from obtaining private gains through acts of injustice to others. The shaping and reshaping of this framework, or system of general laws which all must obey, of course, necessarily and properly affects or modifies, from time to time, the exact limits and areas of all private, economic freedoms and the detailed structure and working of the economy. But decisions upon just, general laws are in nature unlike economic decisions upon the most economically efficient ways of using resources; and different, mental and social processes are needed to yield appropriate decisions of these two different kinds. The pursuit of justice—of agreement or consensus on what the provisions of just laws must be—in general cannot be as simply, largely rational, or logico-empirical, as the pursuit of wealth, within the areas of freedom defined by the laws, can be. Although the collective effort to reach agreement on the rules of justice should emphatically involve that moral use of reason which I spoke of earlier, this necessarily differs from the more largely or nearly applied-scientific use of reason which is possible and desirable in the economic sphere; or involves, even at its best, an admixture with the common effort to approach morally reasonable agreements of an interplay of diverse and conflicting emotions or passions that has an appropriate role in the political but not in the economic sphere. In the search for rules of justice which they can agree on, diversely situated people and groups, with their diverse interests and viewpoints, start with diverse and often conflicting, more or less strongly felt or impassioned views of their own and each other's rights or what justice calls for. And the merit of the democratic political process is that it can allow fair expressions and weights to all such attitudes and enable them all to modify each other and contribute to the eventual, balanced agreements or compromises representing the best attainable approximations to real or ideal, impartial justice. But undue extensions of the work of this process, and the emotional factors inherent in it, into the other sphere of the making or direct control of economic decisions are in general bound to injure or reduce the economic rationality or wisdom of the latter.

Thus if a democratic state undertakes too much in the way of direct control or management of the economy, it will have to carry it out in one or both of two ways, both undesirable. Either the shifting balance of political forces or pressures will directly control governmental economic decisions and make them generally, more or less economically irrational, wasteful, or bad not good for the economic welfare of the people; or, in the effort to prevent this result, the administrative bureaucracy will be enlarged and strengthened, and the making of economic decisions will be entrusted to bureaucratic agencies staffed with "experts" and protected or insulated from political, that is, from democratic control. But the latter procedure is undemocratic and creates a system in which the makers of economic decisions are neither sufficiently controlled by, or responsive

to, the wants or wishes of the people as expressed either
through the political process or through the markets, nor
impelled toward high rationality and efficiency by the
profit and loss incentives, guides, and sanctions which do
act in that direction upon the decisions of the managers of
competing, private enterprises. Thus far, this argument of
mine may seem designed to prove that we should return
all the way to, or readopt, the old, pure, unqualified, *laissez
faire* ideal of no intrusion by the state or government into
the sphere of making or directly controlling economic
decisions; but I do not mean to press the argument that
far. In the conduct of human affairs, it is always necessary
to try to balance, as well as possible, many diverse, opposed
considerations and adopt the middle way or course based
on appropriate, simultaneous appreciations and weightings
of them all. Thus the considerations that I have been urging
against extending the work and authority of the government too far into the economic sphere must be weighed
against all the considerations pointing to real needs for
some such extensions, if we are to find the points or limits
to which they should go and at which they should stop.

The modern sources or grounds of real needs for substantial but limited departures from *laissez faire* in the old,
complete sense are I think of three principal kinds. In the
first place, the structures of our modern, real economies
and societies have perhaps so evolved or changed, away
from close resemblance to the so-called atomistic, competitive model that was in the minds of the old classical, liberal,
political economists, that we have come to need new types

of control or restraint of the increased, monopoly powers
of various, large and strong organizations and organized
groups which no longer are or can be sufficiently controlled
in the public interest by the forces or pressures of market
competition in the classical sense. In the second place, the
business economy as it operates or functions and develops
under pure or almost pure *laissez faire* policies always has
had one major fault or weakness, namely, its tendency to
grow and advance to higher levels of productivity in a
fitful, unsteady way or through a series of alternating booms
or prosperities and ensuing depressions or painful and wasteful readjustments in the system involving widespread unemployment and serious losses and hardships for large numbers
of people. And there has been and is going on in our time
a growth or advance of knowledge in this field that should
make possible—if the governmental policies suggested by
this knowledge as theoretically desirable and feasible can
be shaped and carried out in practice on truly wise or rational lines, or without getting distorted by the vagaries of
democratic politics and bureaucratic gadgetry—sound progress in controlling and moderating, through combined, appropriate, governmental and private efforts, the booms and
depressions or excessive detours around the straight road
of economic progress. And finally, in the third place, I
think we do need some things in the area of the modern
growth of public welfare measures for the benefit of the
unfortunate minority-groups of people whose either in-
nate or environmentally caused deficiencies of ability to
support themselves and prosper adequately through the

market values of the productive services they are able to perform or render make public assistance to them necessary on humane grounds. Besides the need to control the too powerful monopolies and selfish pressure-groups in our society and the need to make our economy more stable and steadily progressive, there is also this need to make full, wise, constructive use of the modern growth of prevalence of humane concern 'for all the weak or handicapped people who need help and should be helped for the sake of both their own and society's welfare. I have talked of the need for more carefully rational public thought and policies and I stand by that, but I also recognize the proper, important role of the not purely rational but also, in the good sense, emotional humane attitudes of sympathy with all who need our sympathetic help. I do not stand with those adherents or defenders of the old-style liberal, libertarian, or individualistic tradition who identify it with the precepts of their hard and cold, unimaginative and unfeeling or unsympathetic "common sense," which at bottom is only the all too common kind of narrow selfishness, or lack of sensitivity to the needs of others. At the same time, the humane sympathies which mainly inspire all sincere "do-gooders" do need and do not always have the concomitant guidance of adequate, realistic, rational-and-empirical knowledge and understanding of the costs and consequences of the various ways of serving the good causes they want served and the conditions of real success in serving them at once effectively and economically.

Now I cannot say much more here about any of the three

fields of public effort to improve conditions in the liberal economy that I have now mentioned: the field of the effort to preserve competition where that is possible, and control the monopolies and monopoloid pressure groups where that is necessary; the field of the effort to achieve more economic stability or a nearer approach to continuous, full employment of all labor and resources and steady or continuous economic progress; and the field of the effort to provide all essential help and additional support for those whose abilities to help and support themselves are insufficient. But perhaps a few further words about each of these great problem areas may help to suggest possible ways of coping with them without allowing a too great intrusion of the political into the sphere of the economic process. With regard to the problems presented by the monopolies and pressure-groups, I think the great need is to minimize the need for, or needed amount of, direct, coercive, public control of their decisions or policies by working to inculcate or develop in the managers of the monopolies and the leaders and members of the organized interest-pressure-groups themselves more enlightened and socially responsible attitudes conducive to self-restraint in the use of their powers. As far as business monopolies, or business firms with degrees of monopoly-power in their markets, are concerned, I think the degree of prevalence of this set of evils in serious magnitudes is rather easily and commonly exaggerated though I do not mean that there are no real problems in this field. Despite all the talk there is about an alleged, modern decline of the prevalence in our economy

of competition in the classical sense, I think most firms
still have to meet enough competition for the public's
patronage from other firms offering goods and services
competitive with theirs, as well as enough other, auto-
matically arising, social or external pressures upon them for
conduct consistent with the public interest, to cause their
own interests and resulting policies to coincide as a rule
at least fairly well or nearly with the courses of best service
to the public and all with whom they have dealings. Insofar
as and in the fields where that is not sufficiently true—where
there are tendencies on the parts of firms and groups of
them to eliminate or avoid or reduce market-competition
or achieve and abuse monopoly-powers—intelligent and
vigorous application or enforcement of our American anti-
trust or antimonopoly laws and public policies has I think
a substantially useful role to play although it is fraught with
many difficulties and cannot be a complete panacea. But
finally, insofar as all of the external pressures fail to oblige
the managements of all business firms to conduct them
properly in the public interest, or leave some in possession
of significant margins of power to exploit their customers,
employees, suppliers, or creditors, or obtain ill-gotten gains
at the expense of others, it still is possible to hope and
work for a development in those management groups of
more decent, enlightened, and socially responsible attitudes,
leading them to take into account in their business policies
the interests of all groups affected by them and seek business
success by the route of earning and keeping the good will
of all and not by the route of extorting the greatest possible

gains from others, at their expense, in all dealings with them.

Actually, as I have said, I do not think that business monopolies represent, today, the greatest menace within our economic society to the freedoms of its individual members and its proper working for their common welfare. The more serious menace lies in the powers and aggressive, acquisitive ambitions of the large, strong labor unions, which extort the gains won for their members not only, nor as a rule in the end mainly, from the firms that employ them but in the end mainly although indirectly from consumers and unorganized workers in other parts of the economy; and through other results of the strategies they use, in many ways impair the orderly, efficient operation and productivity of the economy, the working out of needed adjustments within it, and the stability of the price level or the value of money and the possibility of steady or continuous economic progress. Historically the growth of labor unions and their powers occurred as a response and corrective to the despotic powers that were once possessed and exercised by the owners and managers of large, employing and producing enterprises, and the unions have performed and are still performing legitimate, needed, and useful functions. But their powers, and tendencies to misuse their powers to the detriment of society at large, have grown to the point of reversing the old relation between their members and the rest of us; the unionized workers no longer are under-dogs but are becoming upper-dogs, and the true liberal, universal and impartial, humane spirit now demands not sympathy with and protection of them so much as restraint of them for the sake of the majority now victimized by this minority. Here again, however, any all-out effort to solve this problem entirely or mainly or in any great part through direct, coercive, governmental control of these organizations and their activities, in my opinion, would be very perilous and should not be tried. Our hope must be for a growth of enlightened moderation and responsibility in the leaders and members of the unions, leading them to seek only such gains, and seek them only in such ways, as are consistent with justice to all other groups and with the preservation of a generally well-working, liberal economy.

Now as to public monetary and fiscal policies designed to foster the economy's over-all stability and steady progress, I can say, in the time left, only this. The new, modern, "Keynesian" body of economic theory and policy ideas can be so developed and applied as to involve only a slight and safe and useful departure from strict *laissez faire,* or use of governmental power to influence total spending and demand in the economy and keep it in better balance with the total, potential output of all goods and services. But there are dangers in this undertaking that political demands or pressures and the errors of judgment of those in authority may cause unwise manipulations of the flow of money by the government and lead to continual inflation, unjust redistributions of income and wealth among the people, and excessive growth of the government's role in and power over the economy. How to make and keep the execution of this program careful, limited, conservative, and sound is a difficult problem, but I am not without hope that it can be done. Finally, in the matter of the growth of public welfare measures of assistance to all kinds of very poor or needy and weak, subnormal, or unfortunate persons, we need of course to steer carefully between the extremes of hard-hearted neglect or stinginess and an overlavish redistribution of wealth well-earned and put to better uses by more able and productive people to an enlarged mass of unduly dependent and improvident recipients of this public bounty through an overexpanded and too burdensome welfare state. In the main, we should continue to maintain a society of free, independent, responsible, and self-reliant individuals; an economic system of free, private enterprises and competitive markets, in the main self-regulating; and a liberal-democratic form of government devoting its main efforts to its central task of impartially protecting the just rights and liberties of all, and not enlarging the sphere of its efforts too far beyond that, or taking on too much of the work of managing the economy and directly providing for the economic support and welfare of the people.

INDEX